Call to Action

1 3 5 7 9 10 8 6 4 2

WH Allen, an imprint of Ebury Publishing,
20 Vauxhall Bridge Road,
London SW1V 2SA

WH Allen is part of the Penguin Random House group of companies
whose addresses can be found at global.penguinrandomhouse.com

Grateful acknowledgement to Civitas for agreeing to allow us to
incorporate into this book some of the text and tables which, in an
earlier form, were published in a pamphlet by Civitas, 2014

First published in the United Kingdom by WH Allen in 2015

www.eburypublishing.co.uk

A CIP catalogue record for this book is available from the British Library

ISBN: 9780753556900

Typeset by Palimpsest Book Production Ltd, Falkirk, Stirlingshire
Printed and bound in Great Britain by Clays LTD, St Ives PLC

Penguin Random House is committed to a sustainable future for
our business, our readers and our planet. This book is made from
Forest Stewardship Council® certified paper.

Call to Action

BRITAIN'S ECONOMIC PROBLEMS
AND HOW THEY CAN BE SOLVED

John Mills and Bryan Gould

Introduction

THIS BOOK is a call to action – for radical changes to be made to British economic policy. It explains why the UK economy is much more fragile than is generally recognised and how this situation has come about. It shows why the key assumptions on which UK economic policy has been based are flawed and why the consequent mistakes have been so damaging.

It examines the virtual certainty that the current upturn in GDP cannot be sustained and that whoever forms the government after the next election will be faced with daunting problems. It demonstrates that, without a major shift towards more rational and successful economic policies, we are doomed to face years of very slow or perhaps negative growth, stagnant incomes, rising inequality, increasing debt, greater regional imbalances, high unemployment and relative if not absolute national decline.

The key message is that none of these gloomy prognoses needs to materialise. Entirely feasible changes in policy could produce dramatically more favourable outcomes. If the policies proposed here were adopted, we should be able to achieve a sustained growth rate of 4 to 5% per annum; the balance of payments would no longer be a constraint on expanding the British economy; the government would be relieved from concern about running a deficit; unemployment would fall towards 3%; investment would rise from its currently dismally low level to about the world average and manufacturing as a proportion of GDP would do the same; consumer incomes and expenditure – that is, living standards – would increase every year in real terms, all accompanied by a significant decrease in inequality. Last – but by no means least – all these objectives could be achieved with little or no increase in inflation.

Chapter One identifies the core problems facing the UK economy. We invest too little; our manufacturing base is too small; we have chronic balance of payments problems; we maintain living standards only by increasing debt; and our unsustainable 'recovery' from recession depends almost entirely on consumption and asset inflation.

Chapter Two outlines the mistaken policies that have made it inevitable that the UK economy should perform so poorly. We have allowed our economy to become dangerously unbalanced as our manufacturing base has withered. We have relied far too heavily on the service sector – and particularly financial services

– with the result that productivity growth has languished, while regional and socio-economic inequality has widened. We have sold off assets to sustain a standard of living which we have not earned, running up massive debts in the process. And we have relied on rising asset values to fuel consumption, a policy which clearly cannot be sustained indefinitely.

Chapter Three turns to what needs to be done to rectify these problems. The crucial requirements are to increase both public and private sector investment to somewhere near the international average, and to increase our exporting capacity to a point where we can pay our way in the world. For this to happen, manufacturing and exporting need to be much more profitable; the only way to achieve this objective is to establish, through a much lower exchange rate, a competitive cost base in the UK. An economy rebalanced in this way would make it much easier to resolve our many other problems.

Chapter Four then puts what needs to be done into quantitative form, modelling how the performance of the UK economy could be transformed in as short a period as five years – perhaps between 2015 and 2020 – to enable it to grow on a sustained basis at least as fast as the world average, so that we were no longer falling behind year after year.

Chapter Five reviews all the standard objections to a competitive exchange rate strategy and finds that none of them presents any significant threat to the likely success of the policy. Despite widespread belief to the contrary, devaluation is not rendered ineffectual by inflation; the exchange rate is not fixed immutably by market forces but can be moved to where it needs to be by a determined government; retaliation is unlikely to be a problem; devaluation does not make us poorer, but, on the contrary, invariably produces faster growth; it is not true that we have tried devaluations in the past and they have not worked; on the contrary, although invariably too little and too late, they have always made our economic performance better than it otherwise would have been. There is, in other words, no reason why the UK economy should not respond positively to the new and profitable opportunities provided by improved competitiveness.

Chapter Six takes a wider look at the issues raised in previous chapters. What are the risks of continuing as we are, rather than making the radical changes to economic policy we advocate? In particular, what will be the longer-term political implications of years of stagnation, which is the prospect we face in the absence of radical change?

CHAPTER ONE

The Problems That Need to be Solved

THE RELATIVELY poor performance of the UK economy has a long history. From our pre-eminent position during the first half of the 19th century, when we enjoyed the advantage of being the first country to industrialise, slower than average growth rates have meant that we have lost ground until today our GDP per head is lower than that of more than 20 other countries.[1]

The main factors that account for a growth rate that has been so much lower than in most other parts of the world for so long can be grouped under five headings. First, investment as a proportion of our GDP has been and is much too low. Second, we have allowed our manufacturing base to shrink so that we cannot pay our way in the world. Third, for these and other reasons, we have chronic balance of payments problems. Fourth, in consequence, we are running up far too much debt. Finally, what growth we have depends too heavily on consumption and asset inflation, neither of which is sustainable.

The fact that the policies being pursued by the current government have done nothing to remedy any of these deficiencies means that the present modest improvement in the economy's performance is very unlikely to last. An unsustainable uplift that survives till the 2015 general election may – or may not – turn out to be good politics, but it in no way helps us to find lasting remedies for the fundamental deficiencies underlying the UK's chronically poor economic performance.

Investment

Ever since the beginning of the Industrial Revolution two and a half centuries ago, living standards in the UK and elsewhere have risen very largely as a result of investment in capital assets, particularly industrial plant and equipment; it is this investment that increases output per head and therefore living standards. Some types of investment, particularly in light industry with its typically productivity-enhancing machinery, have always produced much higher returns than elsewhere. A new piece of equipment or a new technology can easily, quickly and directly increase production in a way that is much more difficult to achieve through other measures such as better management and training, while investment in housing and most public infrastructure projects, valuable though they may be in other respects, do not produce the same direct and immediate return in terms of increased output.

The returns on investment in capital assets do not accrue only to those making the investment. They are dispersed throughout the economy, particularly in manufacturing industry, in the form of higher wages, greater profits, increased tax takes and better products. It is this social rate of return or incremental output to capital ratio from productive investment which crucially underpins economic growth.

The UK's problem is that this process of capital accumulation has now ground almost to a complete halt. Instead of investing in our future, we consume much too high a proportion of our national income – and that trend is getting worse. In 2008, the ratio of Gross Domestic Investment to GDP in the UK, measured by the Office for National Statistics (ONS) in the way which was standard until it was recently changed to include additional items such as research and development,[2] was just 16.7%, far below the world average; but by 2013 it had fallen even further to a disastrous 14%. That compares with an international average in 2012 of 23.8%, while the figure for China is 46.1%.[3]

Further international comparisons show how badly the UK performs measured by this crucial yardstick. A recent survey, based on 2012 data, ranked the UK at number 142 – equal with El Salvador – out of the 154 countries rated on how much each devoted to investment as a percentage of GDP.[4] Worse, however, is to come. To calculate how much we are really investing in our future it is necessary to deduct depreciation, otherwise known as Capital Consumption, from the Gross Domestic Investment figure to produce a net rather than a gross figure. In 2012, this measure of depreciation of existing capital assets was running in the UK at 11.4% of GDP,[5] meaning that what we invest in our future is now barely 2.5% of GDP – much less than a tenth of the percentage it is in China.

Even this figure, however, makes no allowance for the fact that the UK's population is growing by about 400,000 a year, taking into account both the indigenous birth rate and net migration.[6] If the total fixed assets in the UK, estimated in 2012 by the Office for National Statistics to have a replacement value of £7.4trn,[7] is divided by the 63.7m mid-year population that year,[8] we arrive at a figure of about £120,000 of accumulated assets for each UK resident. Just to keep up with the UK's rising population, therefore, requires annual new investment of about 400,000 x £120,000, producing a total of £48bn. This is a higher figure than the total net new investment that was actually achieved, which in 2012, for example, amounted to £45bn.[9] On this calculation, there is now no net new investment per head of the population taking place in the UK at all.

This failure to invest goes a long way towards explaining the fact that productivity increases in the UK, having stalled since the crash in 2008, have now sunk to almost zero. The increase in GDP which we are currently seeing – amounting to only 1% per head of the population in 2013 when the 0.7% population increase is deducted from the total of 1.7% – is not the product of increased output per head. It is the result of slightly increased demand pulling more people into the labour force – better than nothing in the short term, but not a process that will continue for long and certainly no substitute for improved productivity.

The bald fact is that our economy is clearly incapable of sustainable growth if there is no investment to support it. Every farmer knows that if he consumes some of his seed corn this year, his crops next year will be smaller. We therefore need urgently to lift the proportion of our GDP applied to investment from its current level to at least somewhere near the 24% world average – an increase whose size demonstrates just how serious are the imbalances which currently handicap our economic performance.

Manufacturing

Manufacturing has a key role to play in the economy in three vitally important respects. One is that productivity increases are very much easier to achieve with the plant and equipment which typify manufacturing operations than it is almost anywhere else in the economy; no other form of economic activity does as much to stimulate incremental and continual innovation. Even in the UK economy, where the environment for manufacturing has been so adverse, just over a third of the total increase in UK value added between 1997 and 2012 came from manufacturing, even as manufacturing fell over the same period from 14.5% of GDP to just 10.7%. A further 23% came from Information and Communications, whose contribution to GDP rose from 3.3 to 6.3% as a result of investment in similarly productivity-enhancing assets. The contribution of the remaining 45% of value added over the period required all of the remaining 82% of economic activity.[10]

A second key contribution made by manufacturing is the provision of higher quality blue-collar jobs of the kind that services have never managed to generate in sufficient quantities. The collapse in the number of manufacturing jobs in the UK – down from 4.3m in 1997 to 2.5m in 2012[11] – has had a major impact on employment prospects and income per head throughout the regions where industry used to be strong. This is a major reason why the North East, one of the poorest regions in the UK, achieved gross value added per head in 2012 of only £16,091, compared to £37,232 in London.[12]

The hollowing out of high-quality manufacturing jobs has also contributed heavily to widening socio-economic inequality. In the mid-1970s, the Gini co-efficient, which measures income inequality (with 0 representing complete equality and 100 where one person gets everything), was just over 23 for the UK, after allowing for taxes and transfers. At the beginning of 2013, it had risen to 36.[13] Comparable figures, recorded from the late 2000s, are 26 for Sweden, 38 for the USA and 48 for Mexico.[14]

Perhaps the greatest significance of manufacturing, however, is the vital part it plays in generating export earnings. Despite the decline in UK manufacturing, it remains the case that about 60% of all our exports are goods rather than services[15] and 80% of all our visible exports are manufactured goods of one sort or another.[16] The current weakness of manufacturing means that our exports are lower than they must be if we are to pay for all the imports we want or need to buy. Perennial balance of payments deficits are the consequence.

In 1972, 32% of the UK's GDP came from manu-facturing.[17] By 1997, the percentage was down to 14.5% and by 2013 it had dropped to 10.4%,[18] compared to about 21% in Germany and 19% in Japan.[19] This is why our record on exporting, which depends heavily on manufactures, has been correspondingly so poor, reflected in both our lower share of world trade and our balance of payments difficulties. In 1950, our share of world trade was 10.7%, but by 2012 it had shrunk by nearly three quarters to 2.6%.[20] Because manufacturing is so strong an element in increased productivity, the money value of its output – computers being a striking case in point – tends to decline relatively, even while the volume of manufactured products increases. But while manufacturing therefore tends, even in a successful manufacturing economy, to account for a lower percentage of GDP than it does in an emerging economy, international comparisons show that if it sinks below about 15% of GDP, foreign payments deficits are the virtually unavoidable consequence.

The Balance of Payments

Our overall balance of payments record tells a similar story. The last time we had a visible surplus was in 1982 and we have not had an overall surplus since 1985.[21] While the UK has done relatively very well on exports of services, on which we have a substantial and important competitive advantage, generating a surplus in 2013 of £78bn, this excellent result was overshadowed by a much larger deficit of £110bn on goods, producing an overall trade deficit that year of £32bn. [22] In 2013, we had a deficit of almost £75bn on manufactures alone.[23]

The net trade deficit of £32bn in 2013 contributed to a total balance of payments deficit of £72bn, accounted for by adding net transfers abroad of £27bn and net income paid abroad of £13bn.[24] The UK's trade deficit, although a negative drag on the economy every year, may not on its own be a large concern, but when the other two major components are taken into account, we arrive at an unmanageably large total, and one which is trending strongly in the wrong direction. By the second half of 2013, the UK economy's total foreign payments deficit was running at 5.5% of GDP and at 6% in 2014[25] one of the highest ratios in the whole of the developed world and on an unsustainable rising trend. Extrapolating from the latest ONS figures, the total deficit may well be as much as £100bn in 2014.[26] Viewed against this background, what are the prospects looking further ahead for each of the components of that total deficit?

Of the three major elements in net transfers abroad, the largest is our net contribution to the European Union, which totalled rather more than £12bn in 2013.[27] The UK's payments to the EU are on a rising trend and the Office for Budget Responsibility (OBR) expects our net contribution to rise by another £10bn over the period 2013–18.[28] Other government transfers, mainly aid payments, amount to a net £8bn, with a further £7bn mostly made up of remittances sent abroad by immigrants to support their families. Net transfers have steadily risen in recent years. They were £10bn in 2003, £14bn by 2008 and by 2013 they had reached £27bn.[29] It seems likely that this upward trend will continue.

The UK's net income from abroad in recent years has exhibited a rather more erratic pattern than the figures for net transfers but again – unfortunately – the figures are moving strongly in the wrong direction. During the 2000s, the net income per year earned by the UK averaged about £17bn, but since 2011, when the figure was a positive £23bn,[30] there has been a very sharp deterioration to a deficit of £5bn in 2012 and £16bn in 2013 and as much as £27bn during the first three quarters of 2014.[31] Part of the reason for this huge swing has been the loss of profit flows as a result of the enormous net sales of UK portfolio assets which have taken place over the past decade and a half. Over the period 2000–10 alone, net sales of UK shares, bonds and property came to a total of £615bn[32] – equivalent to almost half our annual GDP at the time.

Another significant factor appears to be that UK banks, particularly those domiciled in Luxembourg and the Netherlands for tax reasons, have written off large volumes of bad loans, probably contracted mostly in

Spain and Ireland. In 2013, the UK had a £33bn income deficit with the countries in the EU, compared to a deficit of £8bn with the rest of the world.[33] The figures reported so far for the first half of 2014 strongly indicate again that there are few signs of these adverse trends reversing themselves.[34]

This must be a matter of grave concern. In 1980, according to International Monetary Fund (IMF) figures, the UK had assets abroad worth $551bn against liabilities of $508bn, a ratio of 1.085. By 2012 it had fallen to 0.949 – a gap between UK assets and liabilities internationally of $873bn.[35] It is impossible to believe that this trend – and the massive swing of $916bn ($43bn positive to $873bn negative) – has had nothing to do with our falling net income from abroad. As long as we run a balance of payments deficit every year, financed by selling off national assets, this underlying further adverse trend will continue.[36]

All of this means that our long-standing trade deficit on goods is only partially offset by the better figures on services, while the overall trade deficit position is heavily undermined by major further deficits on both transfers and net income from abroad, neither of which looks like diminishing and both of which may well increase further. To finance these deficits, we have either to borrow from abroad, adding to the interest charges we have to pay, or we have to sell UK assets to foreign interests, foregoing the returns on them and increasing our foreign income deficit. We have done both. There is, however, obviously a limit to how long we can go on running up deficits and debts, with little or no growth in prospect, before our creditors lose confidence and demand higher interest rates and deflation to bring the position back under control. It is therefore essential that we take immediate and effective action to prevent the current balance of payments deficit from continuing to operate as a very serious constraint on the UK's economic prospects.

Debt

Ever since the dawn of economic history, borrowing and debt have been unavoidable features of economic activity, oiling the wheels of both commerce and government. Provided debtors are in a position to service their borrowings and to retain the confidence of their creditors, debt is not a problem. Difficulties start to materialise only when these conditions are no longer met and creditors start to doubt the credit-worthiness of the borrowers. For both governments and countries, the danger point arises when debt is accumulating faster than the capacity to service and repay it – in other words when the rate at which debt is rising as a percentage of GDP is higher than the growth rate.

For the period between 1945 and 2008, UK governments succeeded in generating the occasional surplus, while for most years there were modest deficits. As a ratio to GDP, peak deficits were reached in 1975 at 1.7% of GDP, in 1983 at 2.5% but at 7% in 1993.[37] In 1945, as the UK emerged from the Second World War, total government debt was about 240% of GDP[38] but by the early 2000s it had fallen to a little under 40%[39] as a result of inflation eroding the value of the capital sum and economic growth increasing the size of the economy. It then rose slowly to 43% by 2007 before climbing very steeply as the financial crisis broke in 2008. By the end of 2013, gross government debt was 90.6% of GDP[40] and still increasing fast – by about 3% of GDP per annum, this being the difference between the government deficit as a percentage of GDP and a combination of the rate of inflation and the rate of growth.

The big differences between the earlier years and the recent period since 2008, therefore, are first, that inflation has recently been relatively low, averaging about 3% on a Consumer Price Index (CPI) basis but only 2% using the ONS deflator measure;[41] second, that government deficits have been very high – 11.4% in 2009, 10% in 2010, falling to 5.8% in 2013[42] – and third, and perhaps most importantly, that there has been little or no growth. The UK economy is now believed to have recovered to the size it achieved in the first quarter of 2008 only during the third quarter of 2013.[43]

Total government debt as a percentage of GDP is already at historically very high levels, and it will certainly continue to grow if annual deficits increase faster in percentage terms than the economy as a whole. Major efforts have therefore been made to reduce the size of the annual deficit, and in value terms it has fallen from £161bn in 2009 to £93bn in 2013.[44] It is widely thought that some combination of further retrenchment in government expenditure and increased taxation will reduce it to much lower levels. There are two separate ways of viewing how this process might play out and neither of them is encouraging.

First, reducing government expenditure and increasing taxation both have a significantly deflationary impact on the economy. If a serious attempt is made to cut the deficit in this way, there is a major danger that its impact will be to reduce the tax take while increasing welfare expenditure, thus causing the economy to spiral down while the deficit stays stubbornly high. In fact, there has actually been little retrenchment so far, despite the rhetoric to the contrary; UK government expenditure – peaking at 49.7% of GDP in 2009 and falling by 2012 only to 47.5% – has risen every year in money terms since the financial crisis of 2008.[45]

There is, however, also a second and more powerful reason for scepticism about the government's current approach. Across the economy, all borrowing has exactly to equal – as an accounting identity – all lending. There are four major components of borrowing and lending in the economy – by corporations, households, government and from abroad – and they must all balance out. Set out below is a table (Table 1) showing the figures since 2008.

Table 1

All figures are in £m. Net Lending (+) and Net Borrowing (-) by Sector

Year	Public Sector	Corpor- ations	House- holds	Foreign Balance	Net Totals
2008	−70,698	99,559	-40,031	11,172	2
2009	−152,053	110,173	27,779	14,100	−1
2010	−150,084	45,847	64,564	39,674	1
2011	−122,979	65,557	31,229	26,196	3
2012	−137,010	50,925	24,996	61,090	1
2013	−94,350	16,039	−962	75,918	−3,355
2014 Q1, 2 & 3	−77,246	−3,892	−1,766	73,515	−9,389

Source: Table 1. Net Lending by Sector in ONS Statistical Bulletin – *Quarterly National Accounts Q3 2014* and previous editions of the same table. All figures are in £m. Figures for 2013 and 2014 are still being reconciled by ONS and the net totals will also be zero when this process is complete.

Of the four components, the fact that corporations are only just borrowing money from the rest of the economy reflects their current reluctance to invest in the UK, although there is some uplift at the moment, albeit from a very low base.[46] Households, although quite large net lenders while they reduced their indebtedness following the global financial crisis, are a little more buoyant than they were, and are now relatively small-scale net borrowers. Borrowing from the rest of the world (in other words, lending to us from abroad) – reflecting and necessitated by, as we have seen, our mounting balance of payments deficit – is on a strongly upward trend.

In these conditions it is extremely difficult to see how the government deficit – which is to a large extent the residual item, bringing total domestic borrowing into balance with the lending from abroad necessitated by our foreign deficit – can be significantly reduced. This could happen only if there is some combination of corporations investing much more, consumers starting to borrow a great deal more or the balance of payments dramatically improving. An unchanged economic policy stance would mean that none of these is likely to happen, and lending to us from abroad is particularly unlikely to diminish unless there is an improbably large improvement in the UK's foreign payments balance. If borrowing and lending by corporations and households remain at fairly low levels, that leaves only the government deficit to approximate to the lending to us by foreign countries to finance our balance of payments deficit.

It is therefore almost certain that the overall government deficit will remain and must remain at its present size of close to £100bn per annum for as long as our foreign payments deficit remains at or above its current level. This means that the increase in total government debt will continue at its present trend rate of about 3% of GDP per annum, implying that ten years from now total government debt will total about 125% of GDP – far too high for comfort. By contrast, the policies advocated in later sections of this book would entail gross government debt falling by about 4% of GDP per annum, thus dropping to under 60% of GDP over the next decade.

This analysis shows very clearly that the current consensus to the effect that debt must be, and can only be, reduced by cutting public spending is entirely mistaken. The current austerity programme is irrational and self-defeating; its effect is inevitably to reduce tax revenue and therefore to increase the deficit proportionately as GDP growth declines and quite possibly goes into reverse. The consequence is that government debt continues to grow to the point where it is unsustainable. The truth is that the government deficit cannot be effectively addressed unless the trade deficit, to which it is closely tied, is substantially reduced or eliminated as the consequence of the improved competitiveness of our productive sector. That improvement will not only reduce debt but also allow the economy to grow faster so that the deficit and debt both fall as a proportion of GDP.

Asset Inflation

Both of the two main indices of inflation – the CPI which measures prices in the market sector of the economy, and the ONS deflator, which takes account of price and cost movements in the public as well as the private sector, have recently been relatively subdued. Between 2008 and 2013, the CPI rose by an average of 2.9% per annum[47] and the deflator by 1.9%.[48]

Over this period, however, the prices of assets – especially housing, and shares as registered by the FTSE 100 index – have been far more volatile. After the long boom in asset prices during the early 2000s, average house prices in the UK rose by a further 15.6% between the end of 2005 and 2007, fell 16.2% in 2008, continued to fall slowly until 2012 but then started to rise sharply in 2013.[49] By May 2014 they were 10.5% higher than they had been a year earlier while in Greater London house prices followed the same pattern but with much sharper rises – by 20.1% over the same 12 months.[50]

These figures mean that house prices have been rising much faster than incomes, increasing 94% between 2001 and 2011 while earnings rose only 29%. The banks' preference for lending on mortgages rather than for productive investment and the failure to restrain that lending with all its inflationary consequences have meant that there is now an unacceptably unbalanced relationship between average incomes and average house prices. Home ownership has, in consequence, become the preserve only of those with well above-average incomes or of people who already owned a house when the ratio was smaller. This is especially true in London where house prices have soared at the fastest rate in 14 years to an average price of some £470,000.[51] We are seeing the emergence of an older generation that is asset-rich and a young generation that is asset-poor.

Share prices have been even more erratic. The FTSE 100 index peaked at 6,722 in October 2007. It then fell to 3,830 in February 2009 before recovering sharply to 5,909 by March 2010, since when it has climbed fairly steadily. It stood at 6,547 at the end of December 2014.[52] Bearing in mind the unsustainable increase in asset prices that preceded the crisis which broke in 2008, it is probably not unfair to suggest that the assets valuations in 2009 were a good deal more realistic than some of those seen since.

The ratio between the FTSE 100 share prices and earnings, currently at just over 13,[53] is well above its recent average. It is now back to the level it attained during most of the unsustainable boom in the 2000s.[54] The ratio between average house prices and average earnings, at close to 5 by mid-2014,[55] is historically also very high. It is extremely unlikely that both will go on rising in price at a much greater rate than that of the CPI, especially if the economy grows only slowly or not at all.

The recent sharp increases in the value of both houses and shares have much more to do with current very lax monetary policies and the banks' predilection for lending for essentially financial transactions than it has with any sustainable trend increase in their underlying value, although shortages are no doubt also a major factor in the case of housing. It is, however, the increase in these asset values, which has underpinned a large proportion of the 'feel-good' factor, which in turn is responsible, through boosting consumer demand, for the recent increase in GDP. While housing and shares might hold their current value for a time, thus continuing to encourage consumer confidence, this does not provide by itself a secure basis for our economic future.

Overall, therefore, the prospects for the coming years look bleak. Without a radical change in policies, we could very easily follow the Japanese pattern from 1990 onwards with one decade of stagnation following another.[56] We have steadily lost ground economically vis-à-vis the rest of the world ever since the end of the Second World War. Why have we managed to do so badly?

CHAPTER TWO

Mistaken Policies

B RITISH ECONOMIC history has, at least since the end of the Second World War, largely been dominated by our undeniably poor performance compared to the rest of the world. For the first 30 years after 1945, we were comprehensively outpaced by most of the rest of the western world. More recently, as other western countries have made many of the same mistakes as we have, the main competition we face has shifted to the other side of the world, particularly to economies along the Pacific Rim. Whereas in 1945, despite the strains fighting the Second World War, GDP per head in the UK was among the highest in the world, there are today not only well over 20 countries doing better than us, but many more catching us up.[1] This has not happened because of any historical inevitability, but because of policy choices which could and should have been different.

Over-emphasis on the Service Economy

There is an established tendency for all economies, as they become industrialised, to see the proportion of GDP produced by services – as opposed to agriculture and manufacturing – gradually increasing. Productivity in agriculture has now risen to a point where, in western countries, no more than 1–2% of the labour force is employed in farming;[2] the UK is no exception. What is unusual about the UK, however, is the exceptionally high proportion of people employed in services – at a little over 83% – and particularly in financial services which, in 2013, alone accounted for 3.6% of the total UK labour force.[3]

The proportion of GDP accounted for by services has increased in many economies across the globe as the reflection of an important relative price effect. The price of manufactured goods has fallen steeply in comparative terms, as a result of massive productivity increases in the sectors of the economy which produce them; no trend on anything like this scale has occurred in services, where output per head has risen much more slowly. Relying more and more heavily on services as the largest component of GDP therefore implies a significant sacrifice of the productivity-increasing opportunities provided by manufacturing and a consequently sluggish growth in output per head across the economy as a whole.

Reliance on financial services, in particular, imposes further penalties. It is true that we have enjoyed a comparative advantage in this sector, at least for the time being, and that its export performance is far better than in other areas, particularly manufacturing. In 2012, for example, financial services alone generated a £36bn export surplus – about half the £74bn total surplus generated by the whole of the service sector.[4] There are, however, major problems with the heavy reliance of the UK economy on financial services.

First, although the increase in productivity in financial services has been better than in some other sectors, it has not been good enough. Between 1997 and 2012, despite the favour with which financial services were treated by the government over most of this period, output per head in this sector rose by just 2.7% per annum, compared to 4.8% in information and communications and 3.3% in manufacturing.[5] Second, financial services tend to produce jobs that, in both socio-economic and geographical terms, are heavily skewed towards high-income occupations in the South East of the country, thereby adding to regional, socio-economic and occupational inequalities. Third, there must be some doubt about the true value of financial services to the economy if the huge costs of the bank bailouts which have taken place are netted off the gross added value they have generated.

Fourth, despite the impressive net export performance of financial services, support for the City has had a correspondingly negative effect on industry, not least because of the City's historic capacity to attract so much top talent which could have been put to better use elsewhere.[6] Fifth, the policy priority given to the City's interests in the way the economy is run – particularly in respect of monetary, interest rate and exchange rate policies and the light regulation of its activities – often disadvantages other sectors whose importance in aggregate is more significant. The task, therefore, is to reduce the salience of the City in policy-making without compromising the contribution it should make towards wider economic objectives.

Mainly because services have been so much more favoured than manufacturing, we have allowed an enormous divide to open up in the standard of living and life chances generally between both the regions of the UK and between the richest and the poorest socio-economic groups. Recent figures for 2011 show that average gross value added per worker in Greater London was £35,638 compared to £15,842 in the North East.[7] ONS figures for 2012/13 showed that the poorest 20% of the population had average pre-tax household incomes of only £5,500 compared to the top 20% with £81,300, although the disparities were considerably less – at £15,600 and £59,000 respectively – when all taxes and benefits were taken into account.[8]

These trends show no sign of abating as government curbs on welfare payments begin to bite. At one end of the scale, total pay for FTSE directors in 2013 rose 14% to an average of £3.3m each[9] while union-negotiated private sector pay rises to July 2013 averaged just 2.5%, down from 2.9% a year earlier.[10] Some degree of income, wealth and life chances inequality is inevitable, but the UK has become a hugely more unequal society since the mid-1970s when the Gini coefficient was just 23. That figure shot up to around 33 during the years of the Thatcher administration, since when it has hovered at this level through successive governments.[11] The figure at the beginning of 2013 was 36.[12] It had fallen slightly in 2011/12, mainly as a result of at least a temporary reduction in the more egregious financial service sector bonuses, but it is now expected to increase again as a result of government cuts in welfare expenditure[13] and the re-emergence of large bonus payments.

A substantial factor in the recent increase in inequality has been the number of people who are unemployed, a figure partly masked by a succession of changes in the way the number of people without work has been counted.[14] For the period from August to October 2014, the headline unemployment rate was 6.0% of the economically active population – a total of just under 2m people.[15] This, however, is a far cry from the long period from 1946 to 1973 when unemployment in the UK for the whole of these 27 years averaged no more than 2%.[16] Furthermore, as a report published by the Trades Union Congress (TUC) in September 2013 shows,[17] the unemployed total would be much higher if we include those who have dropped out of the labour force because they are caught in benefit traps, have been reclassified as long-term sick or have given up hope of ever getting a job.

If we take all these categories into account, the number of people who would be capable of working if jobs were available for them at reasonable wages is not 2.02m but was estimated in 2013 to have been 4.78m. Furthermore, of the 8m working part-time – currently counted as being employed – as many as 6.2m regard themselves as being under-employed and would like to work full-time or at least for longer and more reliable hours. This level of foregone potential employment is both a huge economic waste of resources and an individual tragedy for all those who would like to make a full contribution to society but are unable to do so.

Short-termism

From the 1970s onwards, the UK enjoyed the uncovenanted and unexpected benefit of North Sea oil and gas; at its peak in 1985, this accounted for 4.6% of world production, contributing 4.5% to UK GDP, while exports alone amounted to 2.7%.[18] This huge bonus might have been used, as it was in Norway, to build up a fund worth $857m in September 2014[19] – for the future when the oil and gas run out. Monetarist doctrine, much in favour at the time, however, insisted that North Sea energy production would inevitably push the exchange rate higher and that this meant, with equal inevitability, that manufacturing would decline.

Accordingly, nothing was done to stop the exchange rate rising to previously unheard-of heights in real terms with the result that the gains from North Sea oil and gas were more than offset by the loss of manufacturing capacity. The fact that no such mechanism operated in Norway was conveniently ignored. While UK manufacturing output plunged, imports flooded in. UK consumers benefited in the short term, in other words, by exploiting an irreplaceable resource, but with no long-term gain.

In a similar instance of short-termism, UK living standards in the 2000s were artificially buttressed as huge numbers of UK assets were sold off to foreign interests. Between 2000 and 2010, net sales of portfolio assets – shares, bonds and property, but excluding direct investment in plant, machinery and buildings – came to a staggering £615bn,[20] equivalent to roughly half of our annual GDP at the time. Our cumulative foreign trade balance deficit over this period – although far too high for comfort at £286bn[21] – was less than half the net inflow of funds from net portfolio asset sales. No wonder that, in response to this inflow of funds from abroad, the pound soared to £1.00 = $2.00, with the result that imports surged upwards as our manufacturing capacity went into a further steep decline. The sale to foreign buyers of our ports and airports, rail franchises and energy companies, football clubs, totemic firms such as Cadbury, swathes of expensive housing and much else besides meant that many key sectors of the economy have passed into foreign hands. We have forfeited the future profit streams they will produce as well as control over research and development budgets and investment planning.

The UK at the moment reflects all too clearly the condition of a society which has fought off relative decline by taking a more and more short-term view of the way ahead. We insist on enjoying a current standard of living which consumes so much of our resource that there is inadequate capacity left to invest in the future. Too many of those running our major companies are more interested in share buy-backs to inflate their share prices and to increase their bonuses rather than in ploughing back profits to secure future growth and competitiveness.[22] Banks are much more willing to lend money on mortgages than for supporting productive industry. And since, both as consumers and as beneficiaries of government expenditure, we spend more than we earn, our indebtedness continues to grow inexorably. We have lost sight of the need to live within our means. We must replace this short-term approach with a longer time horizon if we are to have a sustainable economic future.

Our Unbalanced Economy

As we emphasised earlier, our manufacturing base has eroded to an unsustainable extent. In 1970, 32% of the UK's GDP came from manufacturing.[23] By 1997, the percentage was down to 14.5% and by 2013 it had dropped to 10.4%,[24] compared to about 21% in Germany and 19% in Japan.[25] Three adverse consequences in particular flow from this major change in the composition of UK output.

One is that the decline in UK manufacturing is a leading factor in our chronically rising deficit in foreign trade. This totalled £113bn in 2013 – a much larger figure than the £79bn surplus on services.[26] As goods make up about 60% of our export earnings[27] we have no hope of closing our foreign payments deficit without achieving a better performance in manufacturing. Second, manufacturing provides a much better spread of high-quality, skilled and well-paid blue-collar jobs than is the case with the service sector. Third, manufacturing jobs, especially those generating high wages, were in the past much more widely spread geographically with a stronger manufacturing base than they are now, with a strongly service-based pattern of employment.

If we are to rebalance the UK economy so as to keep pace with the rest of the world over the coming decades, we have to end our reliance on the short-term palliatives to which we have resorted over past decades. Our efforts to achieve growth have relied far too heavily on household spending, currently at a relatively high 62% of GDP,[28] underpinned by asset inflation. This has both encouraged borrowing, which is always vulnerable to interest rate rises, and produced increased inequality as those who own their houses increase their advantage over those who do not.

Reflecting the UK's very low rate of investment, IMF figures show the UK consuming 87.8% of our national output in 2012, compared to a world average of 75.9% and 67.3% for emerging and developing countries.[29] The result is an economy which consumes too much, invests too little and which cannot pay its way in the world. No wonder we need so urgently to rebalance the UK economy towards investment, net exports and a reduced dependence on borrowing from abroad or on selling off assets to foreign interests.

CHAPTER THREE

The Solutions

ISTORICALLY, GOVERNMENTS have always understood that some reasonable fiscal balance has to be achieved so that government expenditure can be financed either by a sustainable combination of taxation, fees and charges on the one hand or by borrowing on the other. Since the Keynesian revolution in the 1930s and 1940s, the significance of monetary policy – interest rates, the money supply and the impact of the fiscal balance on aggregate demand – has been accepted as a vital part of the policy framework for controlling the economy.

Unfortunately, an equally vital component of this process – an exchange rate set at a level which enables us to compete in the world – has largely, and especially in recent times, been ignored. The result has been that government policy has failed to set or achieve clear goals and has instead provided a mass of perverse incentives. Rebalancing the UK economy so that we can keep pace with the rest of the world on a sustainable basis requires a more accurate analysis of where our weaknesses lie and a clearer strategy for remedying them. Such a strategy has two components. First, we must change the incentives provided by the market so that investment, manufacturing, exports and import substitution are made much more profitable and attractive than they are now. Second, we must make sure that the supply side of the economy is capable of responding to the new opportunities that will then be created.

Taking the second requirement first, while there is much to be done on the exchange rate front to provide the right economic incentives needed to rebalance our economy towards much better performance in exports, import substitution and manufacturing, it is important to stress that the lower exchange rate we advocate is, on its own, a necessary but not a sufficient requirement for economic revival. There is also a large supply side agenda which will need to be tackled at the same time. A major increase in manufacturing will require large numbers of staff to be retrained. New production facilities will demand the speedy granting of planning permission, and better infrastructure, particularly roads, rail facilities and high-speed internet connections. Adequate power-generation capacity will need to be available. Much better economic prospects will, hopefully, put much more of a premium on education – something which it is extremely difficult to achieve successfully if large numbers of young people have no jobs awaiting them when they leave school and very poor employment prospects stretching ahead of them.

There will clearly also be a need for finance to be directed away from supporting equity withdrawal based on house price increases and other forms of consumer borrowing towards commercial investment in plant and machinery and working capital. An increase in house building, especially in some parts of the country, and expenditure on public infrastructure, are also urgently needed. While it may well be sensible for the government not to be too prescriptive in determining how the economy should respond to much more favourable economic conditions, it is, in other words, critically important that it puts strategies in place to facilitate the market's capacity to deliver the necessary increase in output.

Making Investment, Manufacturing, Exporting and Import Substitution Profitable

For more than the last few decades the UK has suffered from a major structural problem which has been largely responsible for our relative decline in economic performance compared to other countries. We have run our economy so that the most productive parts are unprofitable and therefore unappealing to both investors and employees, while at the same time ensuring that other components of our economy, with much less to contribute to our long-term economic welfare, have been much better remunerated, sometimes absurdly so. In these circumstances, it is hardly surprising to find that manufacturing and exporting – the crucial generators of rising productivity, living standards and national prosperity – have languished, while occupations such as banking and financial services, with much feebler records of rising output per head, have provided disproportionately large rewards to the relatively small numbers engaged in them.

The evidence for this policy bias is overwhelming. Data quoted in *The Economist* showed that the return on capital employed in manufacturing had fallen by 2012 to less than 5%, compared to over 15% in services.[1] Against this background, manufacturing as a proportion of our national income has, hardly surprisingly, fallen much more rapidly than in many other advanced economies.

There is a simple and straightforward reason why our manufacturing and exporting record is so poor. The UK exchange rate is far too high and this is why the profitability of both manufacturing and exporting manufactured goods has been so consistently inadequate and in many cases non-existent. A recent ONS report[2] published figures showing clearly why this is the case. In the 19 manufacturing sectors covered in the report, the average import content per unit of exports was just under 34%. This means that almost exactly two thirds of all costs were incurred domestically – in sterling. If, as we argue, the parity of the pound is about 50% too high, requiring a devaluation of around one third to make the UK economy truly competitive, this means that two thirds of all our current manufacturing costs are presently charged out to the world at something like 50% more than the world average. If this is correct, it makes UK costs about a third higher than those against which we have to compete. Although, as we make clear, there are always qualifications to be made in the real world, the basic maths is simple. If the costs that go to make up the prices we charge in world markets comprise on average 34% at world prices (the import component) and 66% are domestically incurred, and if those domestically incurred costs are 50% higher than the world average, our competitors sell at 100 while we have to charge 34 +(66 x 150%), which comes to 133.

Some industries and companies can survive this sort of huge price disadvantage and buck the trend. Those that have strong intellectual property rights and branding, exceptionally complicated supply chains, a large amount of accumulated knowledge and skill that is difficult to replicate, or protection from foreign competition – or at least some combination of these advantages – will survive. This is why the UK is relatively successful at producing vehicles and pharmaceuticals, and why we still have aerospace and arms production industries. Other companies which succeed against the odds are niche companies or are exceptionally efficiently managed. In the end, however, it is the average that counts – especially among industries with relatively little protection – and this is why we do so badly. Without sufficient profitability and prospects, both talented management and willing investors remain largely absent. The first key requirement for getting the UK economy back on track, therefore, is to make manufacturing, investment and exporting much more profitable than they are at the moment.

Price Sensitivities

If the key to getting the UK economy to perform better is to provide changed incentives for market participants to encourage them to rebalance the economy, and if the most effective way to do that is to change the exchange rate, we need to know what the impact of different rates might be, particularly on the propensity of the economy to increase or decrease the volume and value of its exports and imports.

These price sensitivities are measured by the elasticity of demand for UK products in foreign markets and for foreign-produced goods in the UK. If the effect of a 1% change in the price of exports is to change the volume of sales by 1%, the elasticity of demand for exports is said to be one – or unity. If the change were to be 2%, the elasticity would be two.

The widely accepted Marshall-Lerner Condition[3] stipulates that, for a lower exchange rate to improve the net trade position, the sum of the elasticities for exports and imports has to be more than one (or greater than unity). Numerous studies have been done on what these elasticities actually are. They all show that it takes some time for the benefits of a lower exchange rate to come through – typically two to three years – but that, given this amount of time for the necessary changes to work their way through, the required elasticity magnitude conditions are easily met. Obviously, the more sensitive exports and imports are to changes in their prices, the more effective a given level of devaluation would be and – other things being equal – the lower the reduction in the parity needed.

One group of studies, based mainly on academic work carried out in the 1980s, showed a UK elasticity of demand for exports of 0.86 and for imports of 0.65, making 1.51 in total.[4] A more recent report, based on data from the early 2000s and published by the IMF in 2010, showed considerably larger elasticities, respectively 1.37 and 1.68, making a total of 3.05.[5]

Those who doubt the efficacy of a big devaluation

will probably point to the relatively modest improvement in the UK's net trade position following the significant fall in sterling between 2007 and 2009, when the pound fell from an average of about £1.00 = $2.00 to $1.50.[6] Although this produced a considerable increase in UK exports over the period 2009–12, at 22.5% by value and 12.4% by volume, this gain was offset by a similar increase in imports – 23.8% and 11.2% respectively – from a higher base, so the overall net trade balance did not improve.[7]

This does not, however, invalidate the basic proposition that price elasticities are large enough to make a substantial difference to our trading performance. A large part of the explanation for the response to the 2007/09 devaluation may well be that, at £1.00 = $1.50, the exchange rate was still much too high to allow for substantial import substitution and competitive export prices, suggesting that, in those circumstances, the elasticities for both exports and imports were considerably lower than if sterling had been at a more competitive level to start with.

It may also reflect the fact that price elasticities of demand vary enormously from one Standard Industrial Classification (SIC) to another. The significance of that for the UK is that the fall in manufacturing as a percentage of GDP from over 30% in 1970 to barely 10% now means that a high proportion of the most tradable products – those immediately saleable consumer goods which are very likely to be the most sensitive to price, or, in other words, those with the greatest price elasticities – we no longer produce.

What remains are largely exports which are the least price sensitive – produced in industries such as the aforementioned arms, aerospace and pharmaceuticals, all of which are heavily protected by intellectual property rights, branding, high levels of experience, complex supply chains and atypical high-level negotiating processes. The price elasticities for this type of product will be relatively low, as is also true of another major export – oil – which is saleable only at the world price.

If this is correct, re-establishing the UK's manufacturing base cannot rely on a predictably linear relationship across the whole cost base between our trading performance and the exchange rate. A small devaluation, of, say, 10% or even 20% from our present level, will not be enough to make the required difference; a much bigger devaluation is now needed if, as a necessary pre-condition for taking full advantage of a lower exchange rate, those industries that can do so by virtue of their price sensitivity are to be brought back into existence.

Those involved in exporting and importing may well also have doubted – with ample justification – whether the new, more competitive exchange rate was going to be maintained. All the same, the relatively disappointing net trade response to the 2007 to 2009 devaluation might be thought to require a more cautious approach to the elasticities than those taken, for example, in the IMF report. In the projections we make later, we accordingly adopt the more prudent assumption that the elasticity of demand for exports is 0.8 and for imports 1.0, giving a combined total of 1.8.

Returns on Investment

All investment involves foregoing current consumption of goods and services to enable more output to be produced in future as a result of the returns on the investments carried out. While this is generally under-stood, it is not nearly so widely appreciated that some kinds of investment are much more effective at producing more output in future than others. While some investments, such as expenditure on housing or roads, produce increases in GDP which are barely higher – and sometimes lower – than the rate of interest paid for the money to finance them, others are much more productive.

That is especially true of investment in light manu-facturing which, particularly in recent years, has enjoyed the added advantage of integrated computerisation so that huge advances in efficiency and hence output per hour have been achieved. This is the explanation of much of the progress made by manufacturing in China and elsewhere in the Pacific Rim. While little of this is seen in British manufacturing, investment of this kind has allowed even advanced manufacturing economies such as Singapore to go on achieving significant growth rates, even though living standards there are now higher than they are in the UK.[8]

The improved returns thereby produced benefit a wider range of people than just those making the investment. These benefits include higher wages paid to those whose productivity increases, larger tax payments made to the government and improvements in product quality. These total increases in output are measured by what is known as the Social Rate of Return (SRoR) or – which is the same thing – the Incremental Output to Capital Ratio (IOCR). If the objective is to provide the necessary investment resources to get the economy to grow faster with the minimum restraint of current living standards, clearly the higher the SRoR or IOCR the better.

The SRoR/IOCR, measured on an annual basis, does not, however, reflect just the increased output produced by each unit of investment; it also depends critically on how quickly the investment starts to produce the return it is capable of achieving. An investment which produces a 50% overall return with a gestation period of only, say, a year is worth much more in terms of growth than one which takes two years – let alone many years – such as constructing the

Channel Tunnel or building HS2. This is not necessarily a decisive argument against long-term investment projects but, if scarce investment resources are diverted to projects that do not produce any kind of return for many years, their contribution towards getting the UK economy to grow more rapidly will be correspondingly very limited over an acceptable time frame.

These are crucially important factors in determining how to lift investment as a proportion of GDP from the currently very low levels seen in the UK. Because the same resources obviously cannot be used for both consumption and investment, consumption – at least as a percentage of GDP – has to fall if investment goes up. It is therefore vital that investment should be directed towards the highest possible returns, so that it then becomes possible both to increase investment as a proportion of GDP and to lift living standards at the same time. That requires investment in those parts of the economy where the returns are large and fast enough to make this combination of outcomes possible.

Manufacturing and exports are crucial in this respect because it is in light industry more than anywhere else that productivity increases are highest and the returns most rapid. A very telling example was the experience in the USA at the end of the 1930s and early 1940s, as its economy was driven by the need for war production out of the very depressed conditions it had experienced for most of the 1930s. Between 1939 and 1944,

US GDP grew by 75%, a compound annual rate of almost 12%. Over the same period, industrial output increased by over 150%, while the number of people employed in manufacturing rose from 10.3m to 17.3m, an increase of just under 70%. Output per head across the board rose by some 7% per annum.[9]

Similar if not quite such spectacular results were achieved in the UK after the 1931 devaluation. Between 1932 and 1937, the UK economy grew cumulatively by just over 3.8% per annum as manufacturing output rose by 48%[10] and the number of those in work rose from 18.7m to 21.4m as 2.7m new jobs were created, half of them in manufacturing.[11] Evidence that returns to investment can be as high as this at least on a temporary basis is buttressed by the result of studies showing that, in the 1960s, the average worldwide incremental output to capital ratio was as high as 25%, peaking at 30% in 1964.[12] It has, of course, unfortunately fallen in recent decades no doubt as a result of the much less favourable growth policies pursued since then by nearly all western countries.

A return on investment of this magnitude is, however, to be found in all rapidly growing economies whose revenues do not depend on the extraction and sale of raw materials but on the kinds of products which light industry produces. It is this factor that explains how countries such as Hong Kong, South Korea, Taiwan and Singapore drove up their living standards to levels which in some cases, such as in Singapore, now exceed those in the western world. China is now following the same path.

There is another key factor. It is much easier to increase light industrial output if there is a large pool of the unemployed to draw into the labour force. This condition applied in the USA and in the UK in the mid-1930s. Rapidly developing countries, on the other hand, tend to have large and inefficient agricultural sectors with much better prospects in industry, again producing large numbers of new workers to move into manufacturing. Paradoxically, a key advantage which the UK now has for raising its growth rate is that we also have a large number of unemployed or under-employed people to draw back into the labour force, another vitally important contribution to what needs to be done.

During the six-year period from 1939 to 1944, the average social rate of return achieved on private invest-ment in the USA was a staggering 194% per annum.[13] In the UK, the peak social rate of return on Gross Domestic Capital Formation during the 1930s was 44% in 1934, although much higher figures – 140% in 1940 and 77% in 1941, again under the stimulus of rearmament – were achieved after the outbreak of the Second World War.[14] The projections in Chapter Four of this book assume that it would be possible for the UK, given the right conditions, to achieve an average return on incremental investment of 50% for a couple of years, before dropping back over the next three years to 30%.

Containing Debt

There is much current concern about the UK economy's accumulating debt – not surprisingly since, as we have explained, the outlook with unchanged policies is for both government debt and that of the country as a whole to go on growing to ever more unsustainable levels. Yet the corporate sector is in a strong financial position; indeed, many of the UK's stronger companies are awash with cash which they cannot at present see any prospect of investing profitably. And while many households are clearly overstretched, as evidenced by the mushrooming of lenders at extortionate rates of interest via payday loans and their equivalents, the household sector as a whole is, as a result of the caution induced by the global financial crisis about equity withdrawal and buying on credit, much less over-borrowed than it was.

The major problem areas are the deficits being incurred year after year by both the government and by the nation as a whole as a result of our inability to pay our way in the world. Yet increasing debt is not necessarily a problem if the capacity to service it and

– in the last analysis – to repay it rises faster than the rate at which it is accumulating. The problem with the UK economy is that that condition is not currently being met. Government debt is rising at a trend rate of about 3% of GDP per annum[15] and will go on doing so, while our foreign payments deficit had already grown to as much as 6% of GDP in 2014.[16] If the best the economy can do is to grow at around 2% per annum, these ratios are clearly not sustainable – and even growth at as much as 2% is likely to peter out before too long.

The twin problems of government debt and our trade deficit are closely linked and must be addressed together. As we have seen, across the economy as a whole, all borrowing has to equal all lending. As long as lending from abroad is needed to finance our balance of payments deficit, and in the absence of heavy borrowing by either the corporate or household sectors, which currently looks very unlikely in the light of the low level of economic activity, the balancing item has to be a large government deficit.

The solution to these problems is readily to hand; it depends, however, on the economy being made to grow, through greater manufacturing and exports, much more rapidly. This would, first, produce far more resources with which to service whatever debt is still being accumulated. Much more importantly, however, it will reduce the reasons for debt being incurred in the first place. Although it may be necessary during the transitional period to faster growth to live with temporarily larger government and balance of payments deficits for a time, much better export performance will allow these gaps to be closed or at least very substantially reduced within a period of a manageable few years. If, in the meantime, businesses start investing to take advantage of improved competitiveness and profitability, and consumers start borrowing as they become more confident in the future, the balancing item in the form of government borrowing will shrink. A rapidly growing economy will produce both more tax revenues and fewer calls on government welfare expenditure.

The solution to our debt problems is not therefore to deflate our economy by the austerity measures advocated across the political spectrum and applied by the present government, but to encourage the economy to grow in a sufficiently balanced way, so that debt is no longer accumulated at least on the present scale. The way ahead is not to cut government expenditure or to raise taxation, with all the unfairness, misery and political unpopularity this will entail, but to use a competitive exchange rate to reduce the balance of payments deficit to manageable proportions. Both government and national borrowing will then simply melt away as problems requiring further government action.

Raising Living Standards

Living standards have been squeezed hard in the UK since the 2008 crash – much harder than is often realised. At least until the third quarter end of 2013, the UK economy was still smaller than it had been during the first quarter of 2008 and it is now only slightly larger.[17] In the meantime, the UK population has risen by about 4%, our net income from abroad has sunk dramatically and our transfers abroad have gone up, all of which has put increasing pressure on disposable incomes in the UK. The sharp and sustained fall in living standards over the past seven years has been both longer and deeper than at any other time in our peacetime history. No wonder most people still feel worse off and that the cost of living in relation to incomes is such a key political issue.

The only solutions at present for dealing with stagnant living standards are to use government powers of taxation, subsidy and price controls to give the impression that these sorts of policies can make a real difference. Logically, however, this cannot be right. The only way to get average living standards up is to get the economy to grow fast enough to offset the dilution in available resources caused by our rising population. Reducing taxes, increasing subsidies or freezing prices is a zero sum game and it is a delusion to think that the net result of policies of this sort will make people better off. If output per head of the population does not go up, the tax lost in one place has to be made up in another. Subsidies have to be paid for by increasing taxation.

There may be a silver lining to the gloomy prognosis that increasing our national income is the only way to raise living standards. It has been difficult to persuade the British electorate that the economic policies put in place over many years are ill founded. That may change as it becomes clear that those policies will inevitably mean continuing high unemployment, increasing inequality, rising debt, stagnant living stand-ards (at best) and relative if not absolute national decline. Alternative policies which would make virtually everyone better off may then become much more appealing than they otherwise would have been.

Reducing Inequality

Even among those who are very well off there is mounting concern about the degree of inequality now experienced in the UK. Some of these problems may be attributable to the long-term trends described at length by Thomas Piketty in his recent book *Capital in the Twenty-First Century*.[18] Much of this phenomenon has, however, little to do with the inevitability of a growing concentration of wealth in fewer hands, but is substantially the result of misguided economic priorities and of the regional differences in living standards brought about by the decline of manufacturing industry.

First, the constraints placed by our chronically weak balance of payments on our ability to expand demand drives up unemployment, which is itself a major cause of inequality. The incomes of those without a job are generally far lower than they would be if they were in work.

Second, unemployment as the result of the decline of manufacturing industry is much more severe in those parts of the country which are consequently de-industrialised, producing very substantial regional inequalities.

Third, weak demand for labour has been a major reason for the fall in the proportion of GDP going to remuneration for work (or wages) as opposed to other forms of income, such as rent, interest and profits. It is no coincidence that the share of GDP going to wages in the UK, which was 57% in 1948, rose to a peak of just over 64% in the early 1970s, before it fell precipitately to just over 51% in the late 1990s, since when it has recovered slightly, hovering round 54%.[19] A similar pattern has been followed in many developed countries, and has hit the least skilled hardest. The International Institute for Labour Studies calculated that in the ten developed countries for which data were available, the wage share fell by 12% for low-skilled workers between the early 1980s and

2005, while it increased by 7% for highly skilled workers.[20]

Fourth, the skewing of remuneration away from the unskilled towards the highly skilled is also the consequence of a loss of international competitiveness. In economies with competitive exchange rates, there are jobs across the whole economy for everyone because wage costs adjusted for both productivity and the exchange rate are competitive with those prevailing internationally. In economies where the exchange rate is too high, that advantage is enjoyed only by those who are exceptionally talented or well educated and trained. The result is that wages are unduly depressed for the least skilled, if they are lucky enough still to have a job at all. The greater the degree of over-valuation, the higher the proportion of our workforce that is priced out of world markets.

The policies we advocate in this book will, by providing jobs in manufacturing at a range of levels, substantially reduce the gradient of inequality currently seen in the UK to something closer to those that prevailed in the 1950s and 1960s.

CHAPTER FOUR

Transforming the Prospects for the UK Economy

I T IS one thing to set out in broad qualitative terms what needs to be done to get the UK economy growing much more rapidly. It is another to identify policies in quantitative terms that can be executed successfully within the term of one parliament. This is the next objective. The plan for achieving this goal is encapsulated in the figures in spreadsheet 1 which is laid out on pages 56 to 59. This chapter cannot avoid including dense and detailed calculations and those preferring to take them on trust may want to make a more selective reading of this chapter. The carefully quantified approach we adopt to showing that the figures we present stack up is, however, central to the case we make.

We start with figures taken from the latest available

ONS *Quarterly National Accounts*, which cover the period to the end of the third quarter of 2014. The spreadsheet is based on the most recently available ONS figures, and covers the projected transitional period from 2015 to 2020. The figures in the spreadsheet are all colour-coded. Those in **black** are ONS figures. Those in **medium tint** are estimates for what might reasonably be expected to be the appropriate figures in the future. Those in **light tint** are calculated from those already there in black and medium tint. Below each of the headings are the four-letter codes used by ONS to identify each of the headings in their statistical tables.

The top band of figures shows the projected position over the next few years in money terms while the band below shows the same figures in real terms, using the projected annual changes in the CPI to move from nominal to real figures. This seems a safer assumption to make than the approach taken recently by the ONS, which assumes a substantial increase in GDP not caught by price increases in the marketed sectors of the economy, as measured by the CPI.

At the bottom of spreadsheet 1 are set out the assumptions on which the figures in the sections above are based. The sensitivity or elasticity of demand for both exports and imports is shown in the spreadsheet, on the basis explained above, as 0.8 for exports and 1.0 for imports. Let us recall that the condition generally accepted as necessary if a devaluation is to improve a country's trade position[1] is that the numerical values of the elasticities of demand for exports and imports has to be more than unity. This condition is clearly comfortably met for the UK in the reports from both 1987 and 2010 already cited, and particularly in the latter. It may be significant, however, that the 2010 IMF report – which covered the early 2000s – showed the elasticity for imports to be numerically much higher than for exports, illustrating how important import substitution is likely to be.

The spreadsheet is based on a projected exchange rate that falls from its early 2015 level of about £1.00 = \$1.50 to £1.00 = \$1.10, with the same reduction applying against all currencies, as from the beginning of 2015 – noting that the sterling/dollar exchange rate had already fallen by January 2015 significantly from the average rate during 2014, which was about \$1.65.[2] The spreadsheet uses calculations showing that a devaluation of this magnitude will be needed to rebalance the UK economy sufficiently towards manufacturing, investment and exports as to provide both the overall growth rate and the improvement in the payments balance required to produce a sustainable future growth path.

As explained in more detail below, a devaluation of this size will be needed to enable household expenditure to increase so that consequential improvements in living standards throughout the transitional period will be achieved – a vital requirement if the change in economic strategy is to be attractive to the electorate. Reducing the external value of the pound from \$1.50 to \$1.10 implies a 27% devaluation, which is slightly smaller than the 28% fall in 1931 against the US dollar, when the UK came off the Gold Exchange Standard.[3] In 1992, when we left the Exchange Rate Mechanism (ERM), the devaluation was about 20%.[4] Our own historical experience and the recent fall in the Japanese yen – from 77.6 to 103.4 yen per US dollar over the 12 months,[5] a reduction of 33% – show clearly that getting the exchange rate down can be achieved by a determined government.

CPI inflation is projected to rise a little from its current level and to stabilise at 3% per annum. It is widely believed that devaluations always produce increased inflation, but this is based on *a priori* assumptions rather than on looking at the experience of advanced and diversified economies such as ours when devaluations occur. Sometimes inflation increases slightly but often it does not – as was the UK's experience, for example, both after the 1931 and 1992 devaluations.[6]

Import prices, of course, have to rise – as does the cost of foreign holidays – if the currency has a lower external value, but strong disinflationary factors will also kick in. With a lower exchange rate, both market interest rates and taxation can be lower. Production

Spreadsheet 1

NATIONAL ACCOUNTS

All figures in £bn at current prices

Income   **Expenditure**

Year	Gross National Income at Market Prices ABMZ	Net Income from Abroad HMBP	GDP at Market Prices YBHA	Taxes less Subsidies NTAP	Gross Value Added at Basic Prices ABML	Households APBP	Non-Profit Institutions ABNV	General Government NMRK	Gross Fixed Capital Formation NPQX	Changes in Inventories ABMP	Net Acquisitions of Valuables NPJO
2010	1,576	17	1,558	158	1,401	953	51	337	250	4	0
2011	1,636	19	1,618	176	1,442	986	53	337	261	3	2
2012	1,650	-5	1,665	179	1,476	1,022	50	344	269	2	2
2013	1,697	-16	1,713	188	1,525	1,060	52	345	282	9	1
2014	1,770	-30	1,800	188	1,612	1,212	53	352	325	6	2
2015	1,898	-30	1,928	188	1,740	1,271	55	370	429	7	2
2016	2,055	-30	2,085	188	1,897	1,362	58	389	436	8	2
2017	2,225	-30	2,255	188	2,067	1,427	61	408	493	9	2
2018	2,409	-30	2,439	188	2,251	1,521	64	429	571	10	2
2019	2,608	-30	2,638	188	2,450	1,637	67	451	642	10	2
2020	2,687	-30	2,717	188	2,529	1,745	70	473	736	10	2

All figures in £bn at

Year	Gross National Income at Market Prices ABMZ	Net Income from Abroad HMBP	GDP at Market Prices YBHA	Taxes less Subsidies NTAP	Gross Value Added at Basic Prices ABML	Households APBP	Non-Profit Institutions ABNV	General Government NMRK	Gross Fixed Capital Formation NPQX	Changes in Inventories ABMP	Net Acquisitions of Valuables NPJO
2010	1,576	17	1,558	158	1,401	953	51	337	250	4	0
2011	1,566	18	1,582	168	1,380	943	51	323	250	3	2
2012	1,536	-5	1,643	167	1,374	952	47	320	250	2	2
2013	1,534	-14	1,548	170	1,378	958	47	312	255	8	1
2014	1,568	-27	1,595	167	1,428	1,074	47	312	288	5	1
2015	1,633	-26	1,658	162	1,497	1,094	48	318	369	6	1
2016	1,716	-25	1,741	157	1,584	1,138	49	325	364	7	1
2017	1,804	-24	1,828	152	1,676	1,157	49	331	400	7	1
2018	1,896	-24	1,920	148	1,772	1,197	50	338	449	8	1
2019	1,993	-23	2,016	144	1,872	1,251	51	344	491	8	1
2020	1,994	-22	2,016	140	1,876	1,295	52	351	546	7	1

AGGREGATES

except where specified

Other Data

Total Domestic Expenditure YBIJ	Total Exports KTMW	Gross Final Expenditure ABMD	Total Imports IKBI	Net Trade	Statistical Discrepancy GIXM	GDP at Market Prices YBHA	Net Transfers Abroad KTNF	Total Foreign Payments Balance	GDP at Constant 2011 Prices ABMI
1,595	447	2,042	484	-37	0	1,558	21	-40	1,591
1,642	499	2,141	523	-24	0	1,618	22	-27	1,618
1,598	501	2,191	535	-34	0	1,655	22	-62	1,628
1,749	516	2,265	550	-34	-2	1,713	28	-77	1,655
1,949	553	2,502	574	-21	0	1,928	29	-100	1,708
2,134	588	2,722	677	-88	0	2,046	30	-148	1,760
2,254	632	2,886	695	-63	0	2,191	31	-124	1,830
2,400	684	3,084	714	-31	0	2,370	32	-92	1,922
2,596	739	3,335	772	-33	0	2,563	33	-96	2,018
2,808	800	3,607	835	-36	0	2,772	34	-99	2,119
3,036	865	3,901	904	-39	0	2,998	35	-103	2,224

constant 2011 prices

Total Domestic Expenditure YBIJ	Total Exports KTMW	Gross Final Expenditure ABMD	Total Imports IKBI	Net Trade	Statistical Discrepancy GIXM	GDP at Market Prices YBHA	Net Transfers Abroad KTNF	Total Foreign Payments Balance
1,595	447	2,042	484	-37	0	1,591	21	-40
1,571	478	2,049	501	-23	0	1,618	21	-26
1,487	466	2,039	498	-32	0	1,628	21	-58
1,581	466	2,047	497	-30	-2	1,655	25	-70
1,727	490	2,217	509	-19	0	1,708	25	-89
1,836	506	2,342	582	-76	0	1,760	25	-127
1,883	528	2,411	581	-53	0	1,830	26	-103
1,946	554	2,501	579	-25	0	1,922	26	-75
2,044	582	2,626	608	-26	0	2,018	26	-75
2,146	611	2,757	639	-27	0	2,119	26	-76
2,253	642	2,895	670	-29	0	2,224	26	-77

ASSUMPTIONS

	£/$ Exchange Rate	Exchange Rate Dilut- ion	CPI Inflation	Deflator	Marginal Social Rate of Return	Export Demand Elasticity	Import Demand Elasticity	Real GDP Growth	Net Trade to Con- sump- tion
2010	1.57	20%	3.3%	2.8%	20.0%	0.8	1.0	1.8%	
2011	1.55	20%	4.5%	2.3%	20.0%	0.8	1.0	1.0%	
2012	1.58	20%	2.8%	1.4%	20.0%	0.8	1.0	0.3%	
2013	1.60	20%	3.0%	3.0%	20.0%	0.8	1.0	1.7%	
2014	1.65	20%	2.0%	2.0%	20.0%	0.8	1.0	3.2%	-20
2015	1.10	20%	3.0%	3.0%	35.0%	0.8	1.0	3.0%	
2016	1.10	20%	3.0%	3.0%	50.0%	0.8	1.0	4.0%	
2017	1.10	20%	3.0%	3.0%	50.0%	0.8	1.0	5.0%	
2018	1.10	20%	3.0%	3.0%	40.0%	0.8	1.0	5.0%	
2019	1.10	20%	3.0%	3.0%	35.0%	0.8	1.0	5.0%	
2020	1.10	20%	3.0%	3.0%	30.0%	0.8	1.0	5.0%	

Sources: Tables A2 and C1 in Quarterly National Statistics 2014 Q3: London. Office for National Statistics, 2014

OUTCOMES	Invest-ment as % of GDP	% Exch Rate Change	Exports as % of GDP	Imports as % of GDP	Manufa-cturing as % of GDP	Foreign Balance as % of GDP	Cumul-ative CPI Rise	Cumul-ative Real GDP Rise	CPI/ Deflator Diff-erence
2010	16.1%		28.7%	31.1%	11.0%	-2.6%	1.000	0.973	0.5%
2011	16.1%	-1%	30.9%	32.3%	11.0%	-1.7%	1.045	0.990	2.2%
2012	16.2%	2%	30.2%	32.3%	10.6%	-3.8%	1.074	1.000	1.4%
2013	16.5%	1%	30.1%	32.1%	10.3%	-4.5%	1.106	1.017	0.0%
2014	16.9%	3%	28.7%	29.8%	11.0%	-5.2%	1.129	1.048	0.0%
2015	20.9%	-33%	28.8%	33.1%	11.7%	-7.2%	1.162	1.089	0.0%
2016	19.9%	0%	28.9%	31.7%	12.3%	-5.6%	1.197	1.144	0.0%
2017	20.8%	0%	28.9%	30.1%	13.4%	-3.9%	1.233	1.201	0.0%
2018	22.3%	0%	28.9%	30.1%	13.9%	-3.7%	1.270	1.261	0.0%
2019	23.2%	0%	28.9%	30.1%	14.2%	-3.6%	1.308	1.324	0.0%
2020	24.6%	0%	28.9%	30.1%	14.7%	-3.4%	1.348	1.324	0.0%

runs increase, resulting in economies of scale and lower costs. Sourcing tends to become more locally based, moving away from now more expensive foreign suppliers. Productivity increases in manufacturing tend to rise sharply as greater investment comes on stream, again reducing costs. All these factors help to generate a wages climate in which moderation tends to prevail, making it more rational for sectional interests not to press their claims too hard. Historical experience nevertheless shows that inflation does tend to be rather higher in fast-growing economies; this is largely the result of an averaging effect, often designated as Leading Sector Inflation, between sectors of the economy where productivity and wages are increasing fast and other areas where higher wages cannot be offset by greater output per head – so provision for some increases in the CPI above 2% would be prudent.

The social rate of return on investment – i.e. not only the direct return to whoever pays for the investment but including all the benefits which flow from it in the form of higher wages and profitability across the economy, increased tax receipts and better quality goods and services – is projected to rise strongly as more investment takes place and unemployment falls steeply. The assumption made in the spreadsheet is that the incremental increase in investment above current levels would have a social rate of return of 50% for a couple of years, falling over the next three years to 30%. Figures as high as this would be possible only if a substantial proportion of new investment is in manufacturing and if there is ample new labour to draw into the labour force, but the feasibility of this being achieved is strongly evidenced in the experience of economies pulling out of conditions where there are large pools of labour available to be drawn into production.

At the top part of the table, Net Income from Abroad is projected to stay negative – at -£30bn per annum – while Net Transfers Abroad are expected to rise slowly, mainly as a result of our increasing net transfers to the European Union, which are projected by the Office for Budget Responsibility to rise to a cumulative total of about £10bn over the period between 2013 and 2018.[7] Net Income from Abroad fell from an average of £21.6bn per annum between 2007 and 2011 to -£5.3bn in 2012 and £15.8bn in 2013 with at least double this figure projected for 2014.[8] As we saw earlier, the main reason for this is a very steep fall in Portfolio Income, largely as a result of the major sell-off of UK assets which took place in the 2000s and since then, combined with a recent fall in Direct Income from Abroad, which appears to be the result of major debt write-offs by UK-owned banks domiciled for tax reasons in countries such as The Netherlands and Luxembourg. Neither of these trends is projected to be reversed in the near future.

To avoid circularity in the spreadsheet, it is then necessary to make assumptions about what the resulting increases year by year in Gross Domestic Product would be and these are set out in the spreadsheet. The increases in GDP have to be consistent, however, with the other figures in the spreadsheet and considerable care has been taken to make sure that they fulfil this requirement.

The crucial issue then is whether, based on the assumptions set out above, it would be possible for the UK economy to shift sufficient resources into investment and exports to keep the foreign payments gap manageable and to get the economy growing at 4 to 5% per annum, while at the same time increasing real living standards and avoiding an unacceptable level of inflation. The spreadsheet indicates that it would be possible for all these objectives to be achieved, taking account of the following factors:

- The impact on export performance from an elasticity of demand for exports of 1.0 is that each 1% reduction in price increases the volume of exports by 1%. The projected figures for exports from 2015 onwards take account of this impact (subject to the points in the following paragraphs), starting with the previous year's figure and then taking account of the change in the exchange rate, the growth in the economy and, in the top band of figures which allow for inflation but not those further down which do not, the rise in the CPI.

- The IMF figures for the sensitivity of export volumes to changes in their price level, reflecting widespread experience referred to as the J-Curve effect, show that it takes two or three years for their impact to be fully felt on the trade balance. For the first year or so, while the economy adjusts to the new price signals, the impact is much less. To allow for the fact that it will take up to three years for the economy to adapt to its more competitive status, the rise in exports as set out in the paragraph above is assumed to take place over a three-year period with one third of the impact being felt each year.

- The impact on imports of an elasticity of demand of 1.0 – again measured in the domestic currency – is that for each 1% reduction in price import volumes will fall by 1% but rise by 1% in value. This means that with an elasticity of, say, 1.0, the reduction in volume and the increase in value cancel each other out, leaving imports by total value the same as they were before, measured in sterling. If the elasticity is not 1.0 – but some other figure such as 1.2 – then the effect of a 1% devaluation would be to reduce import volumes by 1.2% while their value rises by 1.0%, the overall effect being that in this case imports would fall in total value by 0.2%.

- A devaluation of, say, 33%, however, will not change import and export prices by this full percentage. Exporters will use some of the reduction in their costs to improve their margins and importers will react in the opposite way. It is assumed in the spreadsheet, in the light of experience from previous major exchange rate changes of the magnitude contemplated in the spreadsheet, that one fifth of the reduction in the exchange rate will be effectively eroded in this respect for both exports and imports. This is shown in the assumptions in the spreadsheet as 'Exchange Rate Dilution'.

- Historical evidence, demonstrated in the IMF elasticity figures, also suggests strongly that it takes longer for export than import volumes to increase. It is therefore assumed in the spreadsheet that import volumes rise by 10% more than they otherwise would have done in 2015, the year when the devaluation is shown in the spreadsheet as taking place, before increasing by 5% less for the next two years as the impact of the devaluation on import substitution works its way through. This is likely to be the outcome, not least because higher volumes of manufacturing are bound to lead initially to steep increases in the purchase of both capital equipment and raw materials from abroad.

With these assumptions, a devaluation from $1.50 to $1.10 (with equivalent reductions in the value of sterling vis-à-vis other currencies) would remove the foreign payments deficit in three years if no other action was taken. There would be a steep short-term increase in the deficit, which would no doubt help to get the external value of sterling down, before the current account stabilised with a relatively small surplus, allowing for the fact that the trade surplus has to be large enough to cover deficits on Net Income and Transfers. For the reasons set out below, however, there may be strong arguments for taking action to avoid the foreign payments gap closing as fast as this during the transitional period to faster growth.

Taking all these considerations into account, the spreadsheet shows the following intermediate results:

- On the basis of all the assumptions set out above, it would be possible to move towards expanding the economy on a sustainable basis to 5% per annum in real terms. Although increasingly higher productivity increases could be anticipated as investment levels rise, initially productivity might increase at no more than the historical average of about 2% per annum. Much of the early increase in the growth rate would therefore result in a cumulative rise in the demand for labour, which would in turn mean an increase in the size of the number of people employed of about 2% of about 30m – the approximate size of the current UK labour force[9] – or 600,000 per year. Past experience indicates that it is likely that about two thirds of the newly employed would be those previously registered as unemployed and one third would be people drawn into the labour force who had not previously been looking for work.[10] No allowance has been made for increased inward migration; if the UK economy started to perform much better than others in the EU this could well increase the amount of available labour by a further substantial number of potential employees, albeit while putting a further strain on the UK's infrastructure, housing stock and capital assets generally.

- To provide for both increased manufacturing and net trade output requirements as well as increases in demand for capital expenditure from consumers, the voluntary sector and government, it would be necessary to raise gross investment as a proportion of GDP from about 14%, its current level, to well over 20%. This could happen, while still allowing household expenditure to increase by an average of rather more than 3% per annum, with increased GDP providing most but not all of the resources needed to accommodate all these claims on UK economic output at once. As explained in more detail below, however, these outcomes could be achieved at the same time only if the UK continued to run a substantial balance of payments deficit for some years. This would, however, be a strategy which it would be safe to adopt if the economy was both growing fast and it had clearly become more competitive in world trading terms, thus being able to retain its creditworthiness.

- About 45% of all our exports and just under 60% of all our imports are manufactured goods.[11] If export volumes and import substitution are both to be proportionately increased by the necessary amount, the proportion of GDP accounted for by manufacturing in the spreadsheet would rise from 10.4% in 2013 to between 14 and 15% in 2020. This percentage does not, however, allow for the need for the further improvement in net trade required to close the foreign payments gap, so the proportion of GDP derived from manufacturing might have to rise further, to rather more than 15%, if the foreign deficit is to be eliminated, including all the UK's forthcoming transfer commitments and net loss of income from abroad.

To get through the transitional period with manageable figures, a number of additional factors to do with manufacturing need to be taken into account:

- If, as shown in a separate spreadsheet (spreadsheet 2) on page 71, whose figures are linked to spreadsheet 1, the proportion of GDP devoted to manufacturing rises between 2013 and 2020 from 10.3 to 14.7%, this would mean an increase of about 87% in absolute terms, and require manufacturing output to expand at an average of about 10% per annum, while at the same time the economy expands between 2014 and 2020 by 30% in real terms – from £1,708bn to £2,224bn at 2011 prices, at an average of 4.5% per annum. An increase in output of 10% per annum in manufacturing from the current low base should be achievable but, if it is not, the consequent strain on resources could be taken by running a somewhat larger balance of payments deficit for a little longer.

- This rate of growth in manufacturing output depends heavily on the social rate of return (or the incremental output to capital ratio) being high enough. This will happen only if the UK economy combines rapidly reducing unemployment with recapturing a sufficiently substantial amount of the highly productive light industry, with high returns and short gestation periods, which has migrated over recent times to the Pacific Rim. This, in turn, will only occur if the cost base in the UK is charged out at a sufficiently competitive rate, which in turn makes the deep devaluation posited an essential component of the strategy.

- If these very high returns on investment cannot be achieved, at least over the short period when currently unused resources, particularly labour, are pressed into service, the prospects of achieving sustainable high growth become much harder to realise. This is why it is so important to concentrate resources where the returns on investment are highest. This needs to be done by providing appropriate price signals, so that these manufacturing activities become quickly and highly profitable. The lower the social rate of return, the more investment is required for any given rate of growth, the fewer resources are available to reduce or close the foreign payments gap, and the greater the negative impact on current living standards.

- With the outcomes shown in Spreadsheet 1, it should be possible to achieve significant reductions in inequality on two counts. First, a large increase in manufacturing output would disproportionately benefit the regions of the country outside the South East; and, secondly, a tighter labour market would tend to increase the bargaining power of labour, thus bidding up wage levels among those on relatively low pay as more high-productivity employment became available.

If the assumptions on which spreadsheet 1 is based are altered to approximate current policies more closely, it can easily be seen how dismal are the prospects for any government in the UK that takes office without a radical change in current economic policy. Without an expansionist devaluation strategy, growth in the economy is unlikely even to keep up with population growth, leading to stagnant living standards as far ahead as can be envisaged. Even with the proposed devaluation, however, the position remains challenging because of the need to shift so significant a proportion of GDP into investment and net exports without squeezing consumption and living standards. Even with much faster growth and with constraints on public and voluntary sector expenditure, it would take three or four years before increases in consumer expenditure were possible unless countervailing action is taken to deal with this factor.

There is, however, a solution to this problem. Deficits on both foreign payments and government expenditure are unmanageable only if they increase faster than the economy's capacity to service them. If the economy

Spreadsheet 2

	Manufacturing output created/absorbed by:											
Year	Investment as % of Total	Net Total	Plus Exports as % of Total	Net Total	Less Imports as % of Total	Net Total	Consumption as % of Total	Net Total	Total	As % of GDP	Absolute % Increase	Cumulative Increase
2010	25.0%	63	46.0%	206	58%	281	14%	188	175	11.0%		
2011	25.5%	64	46.0%	220	58%	290	14%	184	177	11.0%	1.3%	1.3%
2012	26.0%	65	45.5%	212	58%	289	14%	185	173	10.6%	-2.6%	-1.3%
2013	26.5%	68	44.5%	207	58%	288	14%	184	171	10.3%	-0.9%	-2.2%
2014	27.0%	78	44.0%	216	60%	305	14%	201	189	11.0%	10.2%	7.7%
2015	27.5%	101	44.5%	225	56%	326	14%	204	205	11.7%	8.7%	17.1%
2016	28.0%	102	45.0%	238	56%	325	14%	212	226	12.3%	10.2%	29.0%
2017	28.5%	114	45.5%	252	56%	324	14%	215	257	13.4%	13.9%	46.9%
2018	29.0%	130	46.0%	268	56%	341	14%	222	279	13.9%	8.6%	59.6%
2019	29.5%	145	46.5%	284	56%	358	14%	230	302	14.2%	8.0%	72.4%
2020	30.0%	164	47.0%	302	56%	375	14%	238	328	14.7%	8.6%	87.2%

moves to rapid growth, deficits become far less important and dangerous. The solution, then, to ensuring that household and government expenditure avoid getting squeezed unnecessarily hard – and, indeed, are allowed to grow every year – is to allow borrowing from abroad (i.e. running a payments deficit) to take the strain during whatever transition period turns out to be required.

If the main effects of a much lower exchange rate are to be directed during the transition period not only towards rebalancing the economy towards exports, investment and import substitution, but also to increasing household and government expenditure, the result would nevertheless inevitably be a continuing balance of payments deficit, as reflected in Spreadsheet 1 in the assumptions at the bottom of the table under the column heading 'Net Trade to Consumption'. This points to the need, if consumption is to rise at the same time as investment increases, to continue temporarily our borrowing from abroad, particularly to allow for large increases in imports of plant, machinery and raw materials as production begins to build up. This would necessitate a continuing balance of payments deficit until the time that the economy had achieved the desired rebalancing. That deficit would, however, be – proportionately to GDP – lower in a growing economy than it is at present

To sum up, and on the basis of all the assumptions

made and the calculations based upon them, the outcomes which would then be achievable over a five-year period modelled in Spreadsheet 1 as being from 2015 to 2020 would be the following:

- The growth rate could be stepped up to as much as 5% per annum on a sustainable basis.
- The foreign payments deficit would hover at no more than around 4% of GDP throughout the five-year transition period, except probably with a peak at the beginning which would be helpful in getting the exchange rate down, but at the end of this period it could clearly be made to fall.
- The percentage of GDP devoted to gross investment would rise from its current level of less than 15% to about 24% – close to the world average. This is essential if the economy is to embark on a sustained growth path.
- Manufacturing output as a proportion of GDP would rise from 10.3% in 2013 to close to 15% in 2020, which is moving a long way towards the level needed to achieve reasonably full employment and a foreign payments balance that no longer constrains the expansion of domestic demand. For this to be fully achieved, however, if the objective was to have no balance of payment deficit, manufacturing as a percentage of GDP

would need eventually to rise to rather more than 15%, to take account of the substantial non-trading burdens on our balance of payments to which the UK is committed.

- Consumer expenditure could increase in real terms every year. The projected rise is 18% over the five-year period from 2015 to 2020 – 3.4% per annum cumulatively – but this does not allow for any increase in the population. If the number of people living in the UK continues to rise at around 0.6% per annum, as it has done on average for the last four years,[12] then the increase in GDP per head per year would be rather less than 3% a year. If, as a result of much better economic prospects, the personal savings ratio were to rise from its present very low level, 5.4% of GDP – which is one of the lowest among developed countries[13] – this would make it possible for incomes to rise somewhat faster than household expenditure. At the same time, government and not-for-profit sector expenditure could rise in real terms by 2% per annum.

- Registered unemployment would fall by about 400,000 a year or more for two or three years, bringing the level down towards 3%; the total employed labour force would rise by about 50% more than this, i.e. by an aggregate of 600,000 per year. Increasing the size of the labour force would be a crucial element, buttressed by much higher levels of investment, of the strategy to get the economy to transition to a much higher growth rate.

- It would very probably be difficult to keep inflation as low as 2% but, with appropriate government policies on taxation and interest rates in place, it should be possible to keep average inflation over the period at around 3% – perhaps 4% at worst.

The key conclusion is not only that these figures stack up but that they build in enough flexibility and realism to allow for some disappointments while still achieving better results. The risks involved in adopting a radical policy based on investment, manufacturing exporting and import substitution are therefore relatively low. Those who would like to check either the formulae in spreadsheet 1 or 2 or to test the sensitivity of the results to the assumptions on which they are based are welcome to download the spreadsheet from http://www.poundcampaign.org.uk/media/2020Projections.xlsx.

CHAPTER FIVE

Objections

WHEN PRESENTED with the radical strategy set out above, almost everyone's instinctive reaction is to respond by saying that they do not believe it would be possible for it to be achieved. We are confident that this pessimism is not warranted, and it is clearly important to understand our reasoning. There are six major objections regularly advanced to show supposedly that the policy changes described above would either be impossible to implement or could not be successful. These objections are: that devaluation always produces more inflation, which would rapidly erode any increased competitive advantage that was secured; that governments and central banks cannot adjust exchange rates because they are fixed by market forces over which the authorities have little or no control; that any reduction in the exchange rate will lead to competitive devaluations and possibly to currency wars; that devaluation reduces the real wage and makes everyone in the devaluing country on average worse off; that we have tried devaluations before and they do not work; and that the UK economy lacks the capacity to respond adequately to the stimulus of a lower exchange rate.

The fact that so many people accept in varying degrees some or all of these objections says a great deal about the state of conventional economic thought. It is extremely important that an effective strategy to get the UK economy back on its feet should not be dismissed for reasons that do not stand up to close scrutiny. We accordingly consider each of these objections in turn.

Devaluation and Inflation

It has to be true that any devaluation is bound to make imports more expensive; that is after all an essential part of its purpose. It therefore seems logical that inflation generally must increase if the external value of the currency goes down. If this was the case, however, the historical record would show this pattern regularly occurring. This is not, however, what historical statistics – plenty of which are readily available – generally show. Far from inflation automatically going up after a devaluation, it usually stays where it was and sometimes goes down – as it did, for example, when the UK left the Exchange Rate Mechanism in 1992. In 1991, the UK CPI rose 5.9%; in 1992 by 3.7%, in 1993 by 1.6% and in 1994 by 2.5%.[1]

This is, however, only one example among many others. Even when very large devaluations take place – as with the 72% fall in the value of the peso against the US dollar in Argentina in early 2002 – consumer price increases, which had been almost 26% in 2001, fell to 13.4% in 2002 and to no more than 4.4% in 2003.[2] Table 2 on the following two pages shows the effects on prices of no fewer than nine devaluations, chosen from a wide variety of different periods and countries, to show that the early 1990s UK experience and that of Argentina in the early 2000s are the rule and not the exception.

The reason for this constantly replicated outcome is that while devaluation of course makes imports more expensive, the inflationary stimulus is offset, as we saw earlier, when other factors come into play. One of the key ways of getting the foreign value of the currency down, for example, is temporarily to widen the balance of payments gap by increasing public expenditure and reducing taxation, and two of the best ways of bringing tax rates down are to reduce the rate of VAT and National Insurance charges on earnings, both of which have an immediate dampening effect on increases in the CPI.

Table 2: EXCHANGE RATE CHANGES, CONSUMER PRICES,

THE REAL WAGE, GDP, INDUSTRIAL OUTPUT AND EMPLOYMENT

All figures are year on year percentage changes except for Unemployment

	Year	Cons- umer Prices	Wage Rates	Real Wage Change	GDP Change	Industrial Output Change	Unem- ployment Per Cent
Britain - 31%	1930	-6.0	-0.7	5.3	-0.7	-1.4	11.2
Devaluation against	1931	-5.7	-2.1	3.6	-5.1	-3.6	15.1
the dollar and	1932	-3.3	-1.7	1.6	0.8	0.3	15.6
24% against all	1933	0.0	-0.1	-0.1	2.9	4.0	14.1
currencies in 1931	1934	0.0	1.5	1.5	6.6	5.5	11.9
France - 27%	1956	2.0	9.7	7.7	5.1	9.4	1.1
Devaluation	1957	3.5	8.2	4.7	6.0	8.3	0.8
against all	1958	15.1	12.3	-2.8	2.5	4.5	0.9
currencies in	1959	6.2	6.8	0.6	2.9	3.3	1.3
1957/58	1960	3.5	6.3	2.8	7.0	10.1	1.2
	1961	3.3	9.6	6.3	5.5	4.8	1.1
USA - 28%	1984	4.3	4.0	-0.3	6.2	11.3	7.4
Devaluation	1985	3.6	3.9	0.3	3.2	2.0	7.1
against all	1986	1.9	2.0	0.1	2.9	1.0	6.9
currencies over	1987	3.7	1.8	-1.9	3.1	3.7	6.1
1985/87	1988	4.0	2.8	-1.2	3.9	5.3	5.4
	1989	5.0	2.9	-2.1	2.5	2.6	5.2
Japan - 47%	1989	2.3	3.1	0.8	4.8	5.8	2.3
Revaluation	1990	3.1	3.8	0.7	4.8	4.1	2.1
against all	1991	3.3	3.4	0.1	4.3	1.8	2.1
currencies over	1992	1.7	2.1	0.4	1.4	-6.1	2.2
1990/94	1993	1.3	2.1	0.8	0.1	-4.6	2.5
	1994	0.7	2.3	1.6	0.6	0.7	2.9
Italy - 20%	1990	6.4	7.3	0.9	2.1	-0.6	9.1
Devaluation	1991	6.3	9.8	3.5	1.3	-2.2	8.6
against all	1992	5.2	5.4	0.2	0.9	-0.6	9.0
currencies over	1993	4.5	3.8	-0.7	-1.2	-2.9	10.3
1990/93	1994	4.0	3.5	-0.5	2,2	5.6	11.4
	1995	5.4	3.1	-2.3	2.9	5.4	11.9
Finland - 24%	1990	6.1	9.4	3.3	0.0	-0.1	3.5
Devaluation	1991	4.1	6.4	2.3	-7.1	-9.7	7.6
against all	1992	2.6	3.8	1.2	-3.6	2.2	13.0
currencies over	1993	2.1	3.7	1.6	-1.6	5.5	17.5
1991/93	1994	1.1	7.4	6.3	4.5	10.5	17.4
	1995	1.0	4.7	3.7	5.1	7.8	16.2
Spain - 18%	1991	5.9	8.2	2.3	2.3	-0.7	16.3
Devaluation	1992	5.9	7.7	1.8	0.7	-3.2	18.5
against all	1993	4.6	6.8	2.2	-1.2	-4.4	22.8
currencies over	1994	4.7	4.5	-0.2	2.1	7.5	24.1
1992/94	1995	4.7	4.8	0.1	2.8	4.7	22.9
	1996	3.6	4.8	1.2	2.2	-0.7	22.2

	Year	Consumer Prices	Wage Rates	Real Wage Change	GDP Change	Industrial Output Change	Unemployment Per Cent
Britain – 19%	1990	9.5	9.7	0.2	0.6	-0.4	6.8
Devaluation	1991	5.9	7.8	1.9	-1.5	-3.3	8.4
against all	1992	3.7	11.3	7.6	0.1	0.3	9.7
currencies	1993	1.6	3.2	1.6	2.3	2.2	10.3
in 1992	1994	2.4	3.6	1.2	4.4	5.4	9.6
	1995	3.5	3.1	-0.4	2.8	1.7	8.6
Argentina – 72%	2000	-1.1	1.2	3.3	-0.8	-0.3	14.7
Devaluation	2001	25.9	-2.6	-23.3	-4.4	-7.6	18.1
against all	2002	13.4	1.9	-11.5	-10.9	-10.5	17.5
currencies	2003	4.4	22.0	17.6	8.8	16.2	16.8
early 2002	2004	9.6	23.3	13.7	9.0	10.7	13.6
	2005	10.9	22.8	11.9	9.2	8.5	8.7
Iceland – 50%	2005	4.0	7.2	3.2	7.5	4.6	2.6
Devaluation	2006	6.7	9.8	3.1	4.3	8.4	2.9
against all	2007	5.1	8.6	3.5	5.6	5.2	2.3
currencies over	2008	12.7	8.3	-4.4	1.3	7.0	3.0
2007/2009	2009	12.0	3.6	-8.4	-6.3	-5.9	7.2
	2010	7.1	4.7	-2.4	-4.2		7.6
	2011	4.0					

Sources: Economic Statistics 1900-1983 by Thelma Liesner. London: The Economist 1985. IMF International Financial Statistics Yearbooks, Eurostatistics and British, Argentine and Icelandic official statistics and International Labour Organisation tables.

Further, if one of the usual ways of keeping the exchange rate too strong is to use high interest rates to attract foreign funds, interest rates will be lower if the exchange rate comes down. In the UK at the moment, Bank Rate is very low but market interest rates are not, and getting them down as part of a devaluation strategy is again quite strongly disinflationary. And then, a more rapidly growing economy tends to have longer production runs and greater economies of scale. Investment in light industry produces productivity improvements which soak up wage increases. Domestic suppliers become cheaper than those abroad, mitigating the impact of price rises for raw materials and finished goods bought in from overseas. Importers are also likely to shave their margins to hold on to market share, thus further blunting price rises.

These are the reasons why devaluations do not produce the regularly predicted increase in inflation. Why do so many people nevertheless still firmly believe the contrary? Part of the answer is that it is easier to focus on rising import prices than it is to take into account all the factors which operate in the opposite direction. Another is that monetarist doctrine treats it as an article of faith that devaluations must create inflation to justify their contention that policy cannot influence exchange rates. In turn, courses teaching economics tend to reiterate as conventional wisdom the association of devaluation with inflation, producing a mindset which is seldom challenged, however erroneous it may be. Policy papers, based on careful empirical analysis, have, however, come to a different conclusion, contending that the correlation between depreciation of the currency and inflation is weak,[3] if not non-existent.

Good economic decisions on economic policies are made difficult at the best of times by virtue of the uncertainties always encountered in interpreting the data available. There is absolutely no case for compounding these difficulties by *a priori* assumptions that are easily disproved in this case by examining the historical data.

Changing the Exchange Rate

It cannot be argued that exchange rates cannot be changed because they alter all the time around the world, sometimes by large amounts. The issue is whether these changes arise largely or even exclusively as a result of market forces and whether, therefore, there is in fact little governments can do to get them changed as a matter of policy. The recent experience of Japan, which deliberately reduced its exchange rate against the dollar by one third between the end of September 2012 and the end of April 2013, shows what can be done by a determined government.[4]

Clearly, market forces are a powerful influence and there is a limit to what any government can do to buck market trends. This does not mean, however, that governments are unable to shape market perceptions and to use them to achieve the ends they want. It is one of the strengths of the market that it will react sensitively to the information provided to it. There is no such thing as a 'clean float'; sterling's value is inevitably influenced by a whole range of policies and perceptions over which government has substantial control – issues such as the level of interest rates, the monetary policy stance and whether or not it wishes to see the rate rise or fall and its attitude to capital movements in and out of the economy..

One of the main reasons for sterling's strength, for example, is that government policy has made it exceptionally easy for foreign interests to buy UK portfolio assets, such as shares, bonds and property, compared to what happens elsewhere. These purchases have been on such a scale that the inflow of portfolio capital into the UK has easily exceeded our foreign payments deficit, driving up the pound in the process.

The quickest way to get the pound down would be to reverse these pressures; this could be done by discouraging capital imports, encouraging capital exports and temporarily allowing the current account balance of payments deficit to widen by increasing public expenditure, perhaps mainly on infrastructure projects, and reducing taxation. Direct investment in factory buildings, plant and machinery should surely be encouraged but selling off UK portfolio assets brings no real benefit to the UK at all, other than allowing us to live temporarily beyond our means, to say nothing of further disadvantages such as the loss of UK-based control over research and marketing programmes and over future income streams. The necessary changes are entirely feasible, given the political will to make them happen.

Much would then depend on what the government says about its objectives. If the Chancellor of the

Exchequer made it clear that in the government's view sterling was too strong and that its parity had to be brought down, and that action would be taken on both capital and current accounts to bring this about, the markets would react accordingly.

If the policies set out in earlier sections of this book are to be effective, sterling must not only fall to a much more competitive level but everyone must know that it will stay there, and that it will not be allowed to appreciate as soon as the economy starts to respond with better rates of growth. The required turnaround depends on a consistent exchange rate policy so as to ensure that the UK remains competitive. The government would need to make it absolutely clear that this is what it is determined to achieve.

If the government wants to ensure that the parity of sterling falls from its current about £1.00 = $1.50 to around $1.10, the most direct and effective way would be to announce that government expenditure would be increased, and taxation reduced, with the deliberate intention of widening the balance of payments deficit to whatever extent was necessary to effect the required devaluation. The markets would then have no alternative but to accept the fall in the parity. They would quickly accept it as a new fact of life, particularly if the result was in relatively short order a faster growing and better balanced economy – one that would be better able both to service the debt created by a temporarily widening trade deficit and, in due course, to close the balance of payments gap. The government would need to make clear the rationale behind the policy. The Bank of England would need to co-ordinate its monetary policy on interest rates and the money supply accordingly, and fiscal and supply-side policies would have to be framed to support the new strategy. There would then be no reason to believe that the government could not get the exchange rate down to where it wanted it to be and then to hold it there.

Retaliation

If sterling were to be substantially devalued but our major trading partners were to follow suit, the UK would clearly gain no advantage. Currency wars with rounds of competitive devaluation are certainly to be avoided, but how justified are the oft-expressed fears on this score?

We need first to be realistic as to where we are in terms of competitiveness, and then to explain our position clearly to the rest of the world. Seriously misaligned and over-valued currencies are a major cause of the trade and financial imbalances which threaten international stability. We should straightforwardly explain how far we have lost competitiveness in international markets, how over-valued our currency has become and what needs to be done to remedy the situation.

As we have seen, our share of world trade has fallen continuously and perennially – from 10.7% in 1950 to 2.6% by 2013.[5] We have not had a visible surplus since 1982 and we have not had an overall surplus since 1985.[6] Manufacturing as a share of UK GDP, at 32% in 1970,[7] had dropped by 2013 to 10.4%,[8] so we cannot sell enough to enable us to pay our way in the world. We are, in consequence, running up debts with the rest of the world at a rate which must eventually prove to be unsustainable.

If, in the light of these figures and on grounds of fairness and long-term sustainability, our trading partners are not persuaded of our need for a lower exchange rate, appeals to self-interest may work better. It is not in anyone's interest that the UK should run up debts that we will sooner or later be unable either to service or to repay. Nor is it in the rest of the world's interests that the UK should provide a stagnant rather than an expanding market for its goods; it would, on the contrary, be to their advantage if a growing economy provided them with a larger market and if the goods they buy from us were more reasonably priced.

In addition, we have other factors on our side. Our share of world trade is now so small that it makes little difference what we do, which is why there was no retaliation when sterling fell from its peak of £1.00 =

$2.10 towards the end of 2007 to its trough of $1.36 at the beginning of 2009.[9] Furthermore, the two currencies most likely to be impacted by a major change in the value of sterling have their own reasons for not turning to retaliation. The US dollar is still the world's main reserve currency, so that its parity is considerably more difficult to alter than that of sterling, while the eurozone – preoccupied with so many other concerns – is unlikely to be in a position to do anything effective to counteract a devaluation of sterling.

Finally, a government with strong nerves could easily outflank competitive devaluations if it was really determined to do so. As increased public spending and reduced taxation widened the payments deficit, the case for retaliation would become correspondingly weaker and more difficult and irrational to implement. Retaliation is, in other words, very unlikely but would be a manageable problem if it did materialise on any scale.

Standards of Living

Although it seems that, if sterling is depreciated, living standards in the UK must go down, since our goods and services would be sold at cheaper prices in world terms, this is not what actually happens. The reason for this apparent paradox is that UK living standards are measured in pounds and not in world currencies such as dollars. Although a large sterling devaluation would obviously reduce UK GDP measured in dollars, it would have no immediate effect on UK national income measured in the currency with which UK residents actually do nearly all their shopping, which is sterling. In this vitally important respect, Harold Wilson was right when he told the country after the 1967 devaluation: 'It does not mean that the pound here in Britain, in your pocket or purse or in your bank, has been devalued.'[10]

This factor becomes apparent in the statistics produced by organisations such as the IMF. These show that, almost without exception, devaluing countries subsequently grow and their export performance improves faster in real terms than they otherwise would have done. If population size stays more or less constant but GDP grows, then, as a matter of logic, GDP per head must increase. The notion that a competitive exchange rate strategy implies a 'race to the bottom', with falling real wages needed to compete with the worst of developing world conditions, is the complete opposite of what would actually happen. On the contrary, it is only by pricing into world markets all of our available labour force that productive employment can be secured for almost everyone, with the result that living standards are raised across the board.

The important point to grasp is that we cannot win the race merely by standing at the winning post. If we want to raise wages and living standards in the way that others are doing, we must start where they start – with a competitive economy. By virtue of the stimulus to economic growth that a competitive exchange rate provides, we then give ourselves the chance of keeping pace with or even overtaking them, and raising our living standards across the board, both absolutely and comparatively, in the process.

Some qualifications must, however, be made. If a devaluing country's economy is at nearly full capacity when its currency depreciates, and subsequently a higher proportion of its output is exported, there will have to be some shift in the balance of income distribution towards exports and away from domestic consumption. Also, if investment goes up as a result of better economic prospects, this will have to be reflected somewhere in more savings. In practice, however, these effects tend to be easily accommodated by rising GDP, made all the more likely, as it would be in our case, if the starting point is an economy operating at less than full capacity. That is why, in case after case, the effect of devaluations is to increase living standards. Over the period of the 1992 UK devaluation, for example, the real wage rose by 0.2% in 1990, 1.9% in 1991 and by a remarkable 7.6% in 1992 before falling back to 1.6% in 1993 and 1.2% in 1994.[11]

Experience with Previous Devaluations

The refusal to face the facts of our situation has a long history, characterised by a strong and long-standing penchant for an over-valued currency over a very long period. Two hundred years ago, after the Napoleonic Wars, as a result of the deliberations of the Select Committee on the High Price of Gold Bullion, the UK, unlike almost all the other combatants, went back to the pre-war parity between sterling and gold. The resultant high value for sterling did not cause the UK too much of a problem because during the early stages of industrialisation we had no serious competitors, but when other countries started to catch up we began to lose ground rapidly.

The trend was reinforced when the early 19th-century controversy between the Banking and Currency Schools was won by the hard-money Currency camp, leading to the 1844 Banking Act, which in turn established the framework – again with sterling too strong – for the Gold Standard which lasted until the First World War. Between 1850 and 1914, the UK steadily saw its share of world trade fall and the economy grew more slowly than those of our competitors.

With the onset of the First World War, inflation in the UK was much higher than in the USA, but this did not stop the Cunliffe Committee recommending in 1918 the restoration of the pre-war parity between sterling and the dollar. This goal was finally achieved in 1925, causing the whole of the 1920s to be marred by unemployment, low investment and a feeble rate of growth as the UK's competitive position deteriorated. Typically Cunliffe himself put down one of the committee's dissenting members, a young John Maynard Keynes, opining that 'Mr Keynes, in commercial circles, is not considered to have any knowledge or experience in practical exchange or business problems'.[12]

In 1931, the UK devalued by just over 30% against the dollar and by 24% against all other major currencies[13] with dramatically favourable results. In the five years to 1937, manufacturing output rose by 48%. Between 1932 and 1937 the UK economy grew cumulatively at 3.8% per annum[14] – the fastest rate of growth we have ever achieved over any five-year period, producing a revival of manufacturing capacity that was a major contributor to the outcome of the Second World War.

The UK economy was managed in many respects much better during the Second World War than the First, but by the end of hostilities it was heavily burdened with war debts – particularly the sterling balances owed to Commonwealth countries as a result of wartime expenditure – and with a currency much too strong to be competitive initially against the US dollar and subsequently especially vis-à-vis most of the strongly reviving economies in Europe. The result – yet again – was a falling share of world trade, slower growth and higher inflation than elsewhere.

As inflation mounted in the 1970s, the Keynesian consensus broke up and monetarist ideas took their place. Inflation in the UK fell from its 24.2% year on year peak in 1975[15] although it was by no means wholly quelled. Prices were actually rising slightly faster when Margaret Thatcher left office in 1990 than they were when she became Prime Minister in 1979.[16] The most damaging impact of monetarist policies, however, was on the international competitiveness of the economies which adopted them. The huge rise in interest rates which monetary policies entailed in the UK drove up the exchange rate as the graph on page 94 shows, just as China was adopting entirely the opposite strategy, devaluing between the early 1980s and early 1990s by 75%.[17] The Chinese example was then followed by other Pacific Rim countries which allowed their currencies to fall to much more competitive levels after the 1997 Asian crisis. The Korean won, for example, was devalued against the US dollar between 1996 and 1998 by 42%,[18] and the Malaysian ringgit by 36%.[19] Inevitably, this increased competition from the Far East reinforced the impact of the disastrous period of over-valuation while the UK was in the ERM. There was some recovery after we left it in 1992 but our growth rate was still relatively low compared with many other parts of the world and such progress as was made was clearly too dependent on borrowing and asset inflation. The emphasis placed on trying to keep inflation down to as low as 2% unfortunately required policies whose effect was to keep the exchange rate far too high. After compounding this problem in the 2000s by selling a huge portfolio of UK assets to overseas buyers, we are still left with an over-valued pound, as again the graph on the next page clearly shows.

This sad history of perennial delusion and decline was characterised, not surprisingly, by periodic devaluations, forced upon us when the loss of competitiveness became too damaging to be ignored any longer. Those devaluations were typically a reluctant and partial acknowledgement of a pre-existing over-valuation, and did little more than stop the rot for a time, rather than setting a new and calculated basis of competitiveness from which the economy could grow at a rate commensurate with the success enjoyed by foreign economies.

Even so, our experience of these devaluations provides us with a useful opportunity to consider their impact, and to do so without the usual preconceptions that falsify most conclusions. Setting aside the fall in the value of sterling between 2007 and 2009, there have been three major devaluations of sterling since the end of the Second World War. In 1949, the pound was devalued by 31% against the dollar, from $4.03 to $2.80. In 1967, it fell a further 14%, from $2.80 to

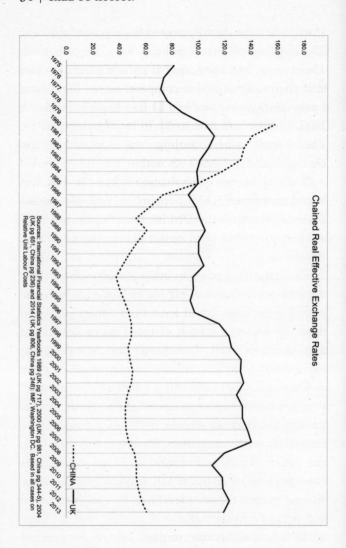

Chained Real Effective Exchange Rates

Sources: International Financial Statistics Yearbooks 1989 (UK pg 717), 2000 (UK pg 981, China pg 236), 2004 (UK pg 651, China pg 236) and 2014 (UK pg 805, China pg 248); IMF, Washington DC. Based in all cases on Relative Unit Labour Costs

CHINA   UK

$2.40. The rate then fluctuated widely over the next 25 years, as monetarist policies were implemented. These were aimed primarily at reducing inflation and little attention was paid to competitiveness. There was a particularly low point of a $1.03 valuation in March 1985, but the rate rose to $1.70 by December 1989. The period when sterling was locked to the Deutschmark at DM 2.95 within the ERM ended with the third major devaluation when the UK was forced out of the ERM in September 1992. The pound fell by 34% against the DM between September 1992 and February 1993[20] and against all currencies by about 19%.[21]

The important point to grasp is that each of these devaluations unquestionably led to higher growth and employment than would have been experienced had they not occurred. Each of these major downward movements in the UK exchange rate, however, was too little and too late, mainly because none of them took anything like sufficient account of the extent of the pre-existing loss of competitiveness and the higher rates of inflation on average in the UK compared to our international competitors. Between 1970 and 2010, the average annual rate of inflation in Switzerland, for example, was 1.6%. In the UK it was 5.6%. Over this 40-year period, the price level rose 88% in Switzerland and by 780% in the UK.[22]

Indeed, it is because sterling was so over-valued

during the 2000s that we have been persuaded that a
£1.00 to $1.50 valuation must be competitive, simply
on the grounds that it is much less than $2.00. Our
continuing decline in share of world trade and our
rising balance of payments deficit demonstrate all too
clearly that this is an illusion. This is not to say that
there was no response to the reduction in sterling's
value. In volume terms, our exports of manufactured
goods grew by 16% between 2009 and 2011 and by
28% by value. The problem was that sterling was still
far too strong and manufacturing too weak for import
substitution to be a major factor. As a result, manufactured
imports rose over the same period by 14% measured by
volume and 19% by value.[23] Even so, these figures show
a significant improvement and were certainly much
better than would have been the position if sterling
had remained at $2 to £1.00.

No Capacity for an Effective Response

Finally, it is argued that, even if a major devaluation was
successfully implemented, making manufacturing and
exporting far more profitable than they are now, the
British economy would not respond. The British, it is
argued, are no good at manufacturing, and there are too
few people with the requisite training and experience
to initiate and manage an industrial revival in the UK.
As a result, we would suffer all the disadvantages of a

lower pound, such as considerably more expensive foreign holidays, to no useful purpose.

This sentiment is largely a function of our long-term experience of a greatly over-valued currency becoming ingrained in the UK psyche as part of the natural order. We are convinced that manufacturing is beyond us and that we are in any case unable to compete against international competition enjoying far lower costs. But, with a much lower exchange rate, these barriers to entry become correspondingly lower. Far from being a very difficult way to make money, manufacturing and exporting would become relatively easy paths to high profitability – as they always have been in economies with competitive exchange rates.

Contrary to conventional wisdom, there is no reason, other than that the cost base here is far too high, why the UK cannot make for itself, and sell to the rest of the world, the vast range of consumer products which are currently imported from Pacific Rim countries. Most light industry requires comparatively little investment to produce high returns, with all the necessary plant, machinery and raw materials readily available from world markets and with intellectual property rights seldom much of a barrier. Nor does most run-of-the-mill relatively low-tech manufacturing – where the big opportunities will lie – require a huge amount of skilled labour, although it will need some.

Entrepreneurial nous and skilled management will,

of course, be needed as well, but there is every reason to believe that sufficiently profitable opportunities will attract those with the required abilities. There is absolutely no evidence that the British are not every bit as entrepreneurial as those in other countries when it comes to seizing those opportunities. This would surely happen, provided it was clear that a sea change in economic policy had taken place, and that sterling was not going to appreciate again as soon as signs of an industrial revival were clearly visible.

Those who still doubt that the UK would for some reason fail to respond to economic opportunities that others have successfully exploited should consider the evidence provided by numerous studies on the sensitivity to changing price signals of manufacturing and exporting performance. The Marshall-Lerner Condition, shows that net trade will necessarily improve, provided that the elasticities of demand for exports and imports sum to more than unity. All the studies which have been produced and published show that when this condition is met, the trade performance improves. Those who believe that the UK economy would be unable to respond positively to a lower exchange rate therefore have to show how that view can be sustained in the face of the mountains of objective evidence to the contrary.

What is true, however, is that the improvement in performance to be achieved from devaluation does depend to a considerable extent on the starting point. As we saw earlier, the sensitivity of manufacturing and exporting to price changes is not linear. With sterling at $1.50 or more, it is still so much more expensive to manufacture most things in the UK than elsewhere that not much improvement in performance will be achieved by, say, a 10% devaluation. It is only with a much larger change in the parity, making it as cheap to produce most manufactures in the UK as in other competing countries, that import substitution and export opportunities really kick in. The elasticities for both exports and imports would then become correspondingly much larger.

Finally, there is a more general and widely believed perception that countries such as the UK, with advanced diversified economies, cannot grow at more than 2 or 3% per annum on a sustained basis because there is not enough new technology to make this possible. This cannot, however, be correct. Reviving manufacturing in the UK does not need to be based on technical breakthroughs. We have wasted far too much time and resources on the forlorn hope that our salvation lies in new technological miracles which will allow us to overtake our competition in one bound. On the contrary, what is needed is extending the use of well-tried existing technology, which is entirely feasible with the stimulus of a cost base that is internationally competitive.

Nor is there any evidence that the returns from investment in these kinds of manufacturing activities decline as GDP per head rises. It is true that there has been a well-established tendency for growth in advanced western economies to slow, compared to the Pacific Rim in recent decades, but this is entirely attributable to the de-industrialisation which those countries have allowed – even encouraged – as a result of their over-valued exchange rates. There is nothing inevitable about this, as economies such as Singapore – now with higher GDP per head than most western countries and still growing apace on the back of a highly competitive export-orientated manufacturing sector – clearly demonstrate.

The real obstacle to the UK adopting the strategy set out in this book is not, therefore, that there are any particularly difficult technical or operational problems to be overcome. It is that for many decades politicians, civil servants, commentators and the academic world have all ignored the crucial impact that exchange rates have on economic performance. It is this that has to change.

CHAPTER SIX

The Bigger Picture

THERE ARE three final comments to be made about the proposals set out above, concerning risk, politics and the future of liberal democracy.

It is bound to be argued that devaluing sterling by nearly 30% from its present level — which is about what would be needed if the strategy outlined in this book is to work — would involve taking a very hazardous step. It is, of course, true that there are always risks associated with any policy change. The key issue, however, is not the chances of the proposed strategy not working out as well as might be hoped; it is whether the risks in keeping the UK's economic strategy unchanged are greater or less than those entailed in making a radical break with the status quo and adopting an expansionist devaluation-led policy.

For there are huge downside risks in leaving things as they are. With no net investment, too small a manufacturing base to provide sufficient to sell to the rest of the world, a large and widening balance of payments gap, rising debt and only unsustainable asset inflation to provide any stimulus, the economy is condemned to stagnate. In these circumstances, it is likely that there will be no increase in living standards, no reduction in unemployment or in the ratio of part-time to full-time jobs, no narrowing of inequality, no improvement (but, rather, decline) in the UK's position in the world. These are not minor considerations. They strike at the core of what most people would regard as a reasonable prospect for the future.

On the other hand, the strategy proposed in this book has reason and common sense, a great deal of historical evidence, and detailed calculations to support it. The risks of it failing are actually surprisingly small. Its success depends on only two variables being in roughly the right place. One is the elasticities of demand for exports and imports in response to changed price signals from a much lower exchange rate. The second is the return on investment which can reasonably be expected to be achieved if it is directed towards those sectors of the economy – primarily light industry – best capable of producing rising productivity and increased output. The values for these two variables in the calculations in Spreadsheet 1 are relatively unambitious compared to what has been achieved both in our own history and many times elsewhere in the world. This means that the policy of which they are a key part is very likely to work. Even if it were to achieve a little less than the calculations suggest, it would still provide a much better outcome than remaining where we are in economic policy terms.

The reason for resistance to a policy with such a high chance of providing a solution to many of our most pressing problems is not, therefore, that the economics are faulty. It is simply that people have been conditioned to believe, against all the evidence, in the benefits of a 'strong pound', in the advantages of cheap imports and holidays abroad, in the supposed inflationary consequences of a lower value for sterling and in the benefits to national prestige from defending the pound's value. Nor is it only the public at large who hold these ill-informed views. They are widely shared among the policy-making thinking class of politicians, commentators, academics and civil servants.

When, however, a newly elected government comes to power in 2015 and looks at the state of the UK economy at that point, the situation may change. No government will want to face the near certainty of unending stagnation and economic failure. This may be the moment when economic policy-makers realise that the conventional view is simply unsustainable – that the risks in undertaking a major change in strategy are substantially lower than the hazards of continuing as we are.

We have surely reached an important watershed in economic policy. Classical economics from the nineteenth century onwards understood the need for sound fiscal policy but denied the possibility of a chronic lack of demand. It took the Keynesian revolution to produce a much better balance between fiscal and monetary policy, leading to the golden period for the West between 1945 and 1970. This was a period, however, when fixed exchange rates and capital controls masked, at least to some extent, the problems to come when liberalisation and globalisation became the norm. Now, as well as ensuring that fiscal and monetary policy point in compatible directions, we – and every other economy – also need to develop an appropriate exchange rate policy and to make sure it is implemented, to ensure that domestic economic policy is meshed with our international relationships. Until fiscal, monetary and exchange rate policies all pull together and point in the same direction, nothing else will work. The chances of this happening will be much increased by a serious policy discussion to establish that a radical change need not be a leap into the unknown, but a bold, rational and carefully calculated response to a difficult but fundamentally manageable situation – a response with a high chance of success. This book is intended to promote just such a discussion.

There is another very important political consideration. No governing class can hold on to power indefinitely if its mismanagement of the country's affairs continues for long enough. Today, we are perilously close to that scenario. Conventional economic wisdom has failed to resolve our problems, and trust and respect for our politicians is withering as a result. The mainstream centre parties are fracturing into relatively small minorities; the pressure is growing on all of them to adopt populist policies which have little prospect of getting the economy to work better. As Adam Smith, the founder of modern economics and the author of *The Wealth of Nations*[1] wisely said, 'There is a great deal of ruin in a nation.'[2] The UK still has huge but not inexhaustible strengths but we cannot go on mismanaging our economic affairs on the current scale without risking a very heavy political as well as economic reverse.

The evident and growing disaffection, in the UK and across the western world, with democracy as a concept, the loss of faith in the capacity of government to resolve our problems, and the dissatisfaction with our political structures are all consequences of our endemic economic failure. They are all manifestations of a debilitating loss of confidence in the virtues of western political and social organisation which has allowed economic disappointment to spill over into a pessimistic conviction that our problems in general are too great to be resolved. If we can successfully address our apparently insoluble economic problems, as we argue is eminently possible by following the strategy we propose, we will do more than raise living standards. We will have created a better integrated and stronger society and a renewed faith in the virtues and values of western civilisation.

About the Authors

BRYAN GOULD

Bryan Gould was a New Zealand Rhodes Scholar who pursued a career in the UK as a diplomat, Oxford law don, television journalist and politician. He was a member of Labour's Shadow Cabinet and contested the Labour Party leadership in 1992. He returned to New Zealand to become Vice-Chancellor of Waikato University in 1994. He has written a number of books on politics and economic policy.

JOHN MILLS

John Mills is an entrepreneur and economist. He is Chairman of John Mills Limited (JML), the company he founded nearly 30 years ago which, based in the UK, sells to some 85 countries across the world. He is the author of eight books and numerous pamphlets, bulletins and articles. He is a lifelong Labour supporter with particular interests in the EU as well as economic policy.

AUTHORS' NOTE

The authors are extremely grateful to Civitas for agreeing to allow us to incorporate into this book much of the text and tables which, in an earlier form, were published in a pamphlet by Civitas in March 2014 and which now make up most of Chapter Four in this book.

Notes

Chapter 1 The Problems That Need to be Solved

1. Wikipedia entry on GDP per head measured on a purchasing power parity basis in 2013.
2. *Impact of changes in the National Accounts and economic commentary for Q2 2014*. London: ONS, September 2014.
3. Wikipedia: list of countries by gross fixed investment as a percentage of GDP.
4. Ibid.
5. *International Financial Statistics 2013*. Washington, DC: IMF, 2014, p. 774.
6. Executive Summary, *2012-based National Population Projections Reference Volume*, London: ONS March 2014. An August 2013 ONS report entitled *Annual Mid-year Population Estimates 2011 and 2012* shows an estimate UK population increase between the midpoint of these two years of 419k.
7. *UK National Accounts Blue Book*. London: ONS, 2013, Table 10.2.
8. *Annual Mid-year Population Estimates, 2011 and 2012*. London: ONS, August 2013.
9. *International Financial Statistics 2013*. Washington, DC: IMF, 2014, p. 774.
10. Figures calculated from unpublished ONS data.
11. *International Financial Statistics 2013*. Washington, DC: IMF, 2014, p. 774.
12. *Regional Gross Value Added (Income Approach) Statistical Bulletin*. London: ONS, December 2013.
13. Wikipedia entry on Income in the UK.
14. Wikipedia listing of Countries by Income Inequality.
15. *Quarterly National Accounts Q4 2013*. London: ONS, Table H1.
16. Table 2.1. – Trade in Goods – in *The Pink Book*. London: ONS, 2013.
17. Quoted in www.economicshelp.org/blog/7617, based on ONS figures.
18. Calculations based on unpublished ONS tables on gross value added by SIC and index numbers in ONS *Quarterly National Accounts Q4 2013*.
19. World Bank Database. Manufacturing value added as a percentage of GDP.

20. *International Financial Statistics 1989, 2000 and 2013*: Washington, DC: IMF.
21. *International Financial Statistics 2000*, p. 982; *International Financial Statistics 2010*, p. 746; *International Financial Statistics 2013*, p. 771 for the latest IMF figures. Washington, DC: IMF.
22. *Balance of Payments, Q3 2014 Statistical Bulletin*. London: ONS December 2014, Table B.
23. Ibid., Table E.
24. Ibid., Table B.
25. *Balance of Payments*: ONS Q3 2014, p. 1.
26. Ibid., Table A.
27. *Balance of Payments, Q2 2014 Statistical Bulletin*. London: ONS, March 2014, Table H.
28. December 2013 OBR report to the Treasury *Economic and Fiscal Output*, Para 4.114 and Table 4.28.
29. *The Pink Book 2013*. London: ONS, 2013, Figure 1.4.
30. *The Pink Book 2013*. London: ONS, 2013, Figure 1.3.
31. *Balance of Payments, Q3 2014 Statistical Bulletin*. London: ONS, December 2014, Table G.
32. *The Pink Book 2011*. London: ONS, 2011, Table 7.1.
33. *The Pink Book 2013*. London: ONS, 2013, Table 9.1.
34. *Balance of Payments, Q2 2014 Statistical Bulletin*. London: ONS, September 2014, Table G.
35. *International Financial Statistics 2013*. Washington, DC: IMF 2014, p. 773.
36. To be fair, it should be said that ONS figures do not present quite such a bad picture although they too show a substantial deterioration. See *Impact of changes in the National Accounts and economic commentary for Q2 2014*. London: ONS, September 2014, Figure 20.
37. *International Financial Statistics 2000*. Washington, DC, IMF 2001, pp. 984 and 985.
38. Website www.ukpublicspending.co.uk
39. *EU Government Deficit and Debt Return, March 2014*. London: ONS, 2014, Figure 1, p. 4.
40. Ibid., Latest Figures, p. 1.
41. *International Financial Statistics 2013*. Washington, DC: IMF 2014, pp. 65 and 79.
42. Ibid., Table 1, p. 3.
43. *Quarterly National Accounts Q2 2014*. London: ONS, September 2014, p. 4.
44. *EU Government Deficit and Debt Return, March 2014*. London: ONS, 2014, Table 1, p. 3.
45. *International Statistics 2013*. Washington, DC: IMF 2014, pp. 773 and 774.

46. *Quarterly National Accounts Q3 2014 Q4*. London: ONS, December 2014, Table F.
47. *International Financial Statistics 2013*. Washington, DC: IMF 2014 p. 65; and calculations from Table A2 in *Quarterly National Accounts Q4 2013*. London: ONS, 2014.
48. *International Financial Statistics 2013*. Washington, DC: IMF, 2014, p. 64; and *Consumer Price Inflation 2014*. London: ONS, 2014.
49. www.lloydsbankinggroup.com
50. ONS report, May 2014.
51. Land Registry data, September 2014.
52. http.//finance.yahoo.com/q/hp?s= %5EFTSE+Historical+Prices
53. http://ftse.co.uk/objects/csv_tp_table.jsp?infoCode=NGUK&theseFilt ers=&csvAll=&1
54. http://fingfx.thomsonreuters.com/2012/02/21/113745ala3.htm
55. http://www.economicshelp.org website.
56. *International Financial Statistics 2000*, p. 165; and *International Financial Statistics 2013*, p. 77. Washington, DC: IMF, 2001 and 2014.

Chapter 2 Mistaken Policies

1. Wikipedia entries on income per head.
2. *CIA World Factbook* – Labor Force by Occupation.
3. ONS data on Employment by Standard Industrial Classification.
4. *The Pink Book*. London: ONS, 2013, Table 3.1.
5. Unpublished ONS tables on gross value added and employees by SIC.
6. Bank for International Settlements 2013 report: *Why does financial sector growth crowd out real economic growth?*
7. Page 2 in ONS regional gross value added by SIC. www.ons.gov.uk/ ons/rel/regional-accounts-gross-value-added-income-approach-/ december 2012/stb-regional-gva-2011.html
8. ONS infographic showing the effects of taxes and benefits on household income, 2012/13.
9. Report produced incomes Data Services reported in *Tribune*, 29 Nov–19 Dec 2013 edition.
10. Labour Research Department reported in *Tribune*, 29 Nov–19 Dec 2013 edition.
11. Graph in www.progressorcollapse.com/wp-content/
12. Wikipedia entry on Income in the UK.
13. www.theguardian.com/UK-news/2013/jul/10/income-gap-narrowst-margin-25
14. Christina Beatty, Steve Fothergill and Tony Gore, *The real level of unemployment 2012*. Sheffield Hallam University Centre for Regional Economic and Social Research.

15. ONS Labour Market Statistics, December 2014.
16. http://socialdemocracy21stcentury.blogspot.co.uk/2013/02/uk-unem-ployment
17. TUC report dated 5 September 2013 – ref www.tuc.org.uk/economic-issues/economic analysis/labour-market
18. Roger E. Backhouse, *Applied UK Macroeconomics*. Oxford: Basil Blackwell, 1991, Chapter 9.
19. Wikipedia entry on Government Pension Fund of Norway.
20. *The Pink Book*. London: ONS, 2011, Table 7.1.
21. *The Pink Book*. London: ONS, 2012, Table 1.1.
22. Andrew Smithers, *The Road to Recovery: How and why economic policy must change*. London: Wiley, 2013.
23. Quoted in www.economicshelp.org/blog/7617, based on ONS figures.
24. *Quarterly National Accounts Q2 2014*. London: ONS, 2014, Table A2.
25. World Bank Database. Manufacturing value added as % of GDP.
26. *Quarterly National Accounts Q3 2014*. London: ONS, December 2014, Table H1.
27. Ibid., Table H1.
28. *The Economist*. 30 November 2013, p. 28.
29. *International Financial Statistics 2013*. Washington, DC: IMF, 2013, p. 84.

Chapter 3 The Solutions

1. *The Economist*. 20 April 2013, p. 27.
2. *Economic Review, March 2014*. London: ONS, 2014, p. 7.
3. Wikipedia entry on the Marshall-Lerner Condition.
4. *Does Exchange Rate Policy Matter?* Published in *European Economic Review*, vol. 30, 1987, p. 377.
5. Export Supply Elasticities, Table 2, p. 21, and Import Demand Elasticities, Table 1, p. 15, in Stephen Tokarick, *A Method for Calculating Export Supply and Import Demand Elasticities*. IMF working paper WP/10/180. Washington, DC: IMF, 2010
6. *International Financial Statistics 2013*. Washington, DC: IMF, 2014, p. 770.
7. *Quarterly National Accounts Q1 2013*. London: ONS, 2013, Tables H1 and H2.
8. Wikipedia entry on List of Countries by GDP Per Capita and page 77 in *International Financial statistics 2013*. Washington, DC: IMF, 2014.
9. Thelma Liesner, *Economic Statistics 1900–1983*. London: *The Economist*, 1985, Tables US.1, US.2, US.7 and US.9.
10. Ibid., Table UK.2.
11. Ibid., Table UK.9.
12. Wikipedia entry on Incremental Output to Capital Ratios.

13. Thelma Liesner, *Economic Statistics 1900–1983*. London: *The Economist*, 1985, Tables US.1 and US.4.

14. Ibid., Table UK.1.

15. In 2013, the government deficit was 5.8% of GDP, but its growth as a percentage of GDP was reduced to 2.9% by inflation running at 1.8% and economic growth by 1.7%.

16. *Quarterly National Accounts Q3 2014*. London: ONS, December 2014, Table 1.

17. *Impact of changes in the National Accounts and economic commentary for Q2 2014*. London: ONS, September 2014, Section 2.3.

18. Thomas Piketty, *Capital in the Twenty-First Century*. Boston, Mass: Harvard University Press, 2014.

19. http://blogs.lse.ac.uk/politicsandpolicy/files/2013/08Reed-fig-1.png

20. *The fall in the labour income share*. Geneva: International Labour Office, 2011, p. 43.

Chapter 4 Transforming the Prospects for the UK Economy

1. Wikipedia entry on the Marshall-Lerner Condition.

2. www.reuters.com/business/currencies

3. Thelma Liesner, *Economic Statistics 1900–1983*. London: *The Economist*, 1985, Table UK.15.

4. *International Financial Statistics 2000*. Washington, DC: IMF, 2001, p. 981.

5. www.bloomberg.com

6. Consumer prices in the UK fell by 6% in 1930, by 5.7% in 1931 and 3.3% in 1932 before stabilising at zero inflation in 1933 and 1934. The CPI rose 9.5% in 1990, 5.9% in 1991, 3.7% in 1992, 1.6% in 1993 and 2.5% in 1993. Sources: Thelma Liesner, *Economic Statistics 1900–1983*. London: *The Economist*, 1985, Table UK.7; and *International Financial Statistics 2000*. Washington, DC: IMF, 2000, p. 125.

7. The December 2013 Office for Budget Responsibility report to the Treasury, Para 4.114 and Table 4.28.

8. *Balance of Payments Q3 2014*. ONS: London, December 2014, Table B.

9. ONS Labour Market Statistics for July 2014 showed the total employed labour force to be 30.61m.

10. ILO Labour Force Surveys.

11. *The Pink Book*. London: ONS, 2013, Table 1.2.

12. ONS Revised Mid-year Population Estimates, 2001 to 2010, published 17 December 2013.

13. www.gfmag.com

Chapter 5 Objections

1. *International Financial Statistics 2000.* Washington, DC: IMF, 2001, p. 123.
2. Argentine official statistics.
3. José Manuel Campa and Linda S. Goldberg, *Distribution Margins, Imported Inputs and the Sensitivity of the CPI to Exchange Rates.* Staff Report no. 247. New York: Federal Reserve Bank, 2006.
4. *Currency Devaluation – How to Get Away With It.* CNBC: www.cnbc.com/id/100725315
5. *International Financial Statistics 1989, 2000 and 2013*: IMF, Washington, DC.
6. *International Financial Statistics 2000.* Washington, DC: IMF, 2001, p. 982.
7. Quoted in www.economicshelp.org/blog/7617, based on ONS figures.
8. Calculations based on unpublished ONS tables on gross value added by SIC and index numbers in ONS *Quarterly National Accounts Q4 2013.*
9. http:fxtop.com/en/historical-exchange-rates
10. BBC 'Wilson defends "pound in our pocket"', available at: http://news.bbc.co.uk/onthisday/hi/dates/stories/november/19/newsid_3208000/3208396.stm [Accessed 09/08/2013]
11. Table 2, p.79.
12. Wikipedia entry on Walter Cunliffe, First Baron Cunliffe.
13. Thelma Liesner, *Economic Statistics 1900–1983.* London: The Economist, 1985, Table UK.15.
14. Ibid., Table UK.2.
15. www.thisismoney
16. Professor Tim Congdon points out that the rate of inflation, measured by the Retail Price Index, was 10.1% when Margaret Thatcher came to power in 1989 and 10.9% when she resigned in 1990. See his article: 'Whatever the folklore, Lady Thatcher did indeed commit a U-turn when it came to anti-inflation policy', IFS School of Finance, available at: http://fw.ifslearning.ac.uk/Archive/2013/june/features/howitreallyturnedout.aspx
17. The indices for exchange rates for both the UK and China are indexed to 100 in 1985 but this does not necessarily imply that they were equally competitive at this point.
18. Page 401 in *International Financial Statistics Yearbook.* Washington, DC: IMF, 2004.
19. Ibid. page 440.
20. 'Oanda' Historical Exchange Rates, available at: http://www.oanda.com/currency/historical-rates/
21. *International Financial Statistics Yearbook 2000.* Washington, DC: IMF, p. 981.
22. Multiple IMF and Swiss data sources were used to compile these figures.
23. *The Pink Book.* London: ONS, 2012, pp. 40–42, Tables 2.1 and 2.2.

Chapter 6 The Bigger Picture

1. Adam Smith, *An Inquiry into the Nature and Causes of the Wealth of Nations*. First published in 1776.
2. Adam Smith's response to Sir John Sinclair, when told of the surrender in October 1777 of British forces at Saratoga during the American War of Independence.